THE SAVING WORK OF CHRIST
SERMONS BY SAINT GREGORY PALAMAS

Michael R. Marsh

THE SAVING WORK *of* CHRIST
Sermons by Saint Gregory Palamas

edited by
Christopher Veniamin

MOUNT THABOR PUBLISHING
2008

THE SAVING WORK OF CHRIST: SERMONS BY SAINT GREGORY PALAMAS
Copyright © 2008 by The Stavropegic Monastery of St. John the Baptist, Essex, UK

First edition 2008

Mount Thabor Publishing
184 Saint Tikhon's Road
Waymart, PA 18472-4521 USA

www.thaborian.com

Printed in the United States of America

All rights reserved. No part of this publication may be reproduced, stored in a retrieval system, or transmitted, in any form or by any means, electronic, mechanical, photocopying, recording, or otherwise, without the prior permission of Mount Thabor Publishing.

Library of Congress Cataloging-in-Publication Data

Gregory Palamas, Saint, 1296-1359.
[Sermons. English]
The saving work of Christ : sermons by Saint Gregory Palamas / edited by Christopher Veniamin. -- 1st ed.
    p. cm. -- (Sermons by Saint Gregory Palamas ; v. 2)
ISBN 978-0-9774983-5-2
1. Jesus Christ--Biography--Sermons--Early works to 1800. 2. Church year sermons--Early works to 1800. 3. Orthodox Eastern Church--Sermons--Early works to 1800. I. Veniamin, Christopher, 1958- II. Title.
BT306.33.G7413 2008
252'.019--dc22
                                2008039637

Front cover:
Theophan the Greek (c. 1330–1410). Transfiguration from Preslav. Russian Icon. c. 1403
Photo Credit : Scala / Art Resource, NY
Tretyakov Gallery, Moscow, Russia

Archimandrite Sophrony
(1896 – 1993)
in memoriam aeternam

Saint Gregory Palamas
(1296–1359)
Chapel of the Holy Unmercenary Physicians
Vatopedi Monastery, Mount Athos

Luminary of the Orthodox faith,
support of the Church and teacher,
splendour of monastics,
invincible champion of theologians,
O wonderworker Gregory,
boast of Thessalonica,
preacher of grace,
pray without ceasing
that our souls be saved.

Dismissal Hymn (Apolytikion) of the Saint
Fourth Plagial (Tone Eight), Second Sunday in Great Lent

Contents

Foreword
xi

On Christmas
1

On the Presentation
10

On Epiphany I
19

On Epiphany II
28

On the Transfiguration I
39

On the Transfiguration II
48

On Palm Sunday
57

On the Precious and Life-giving Cross
65

On Redemption
80

On the Sabbath and the Lord's Day
101

On the Ascension of Christ I
112

On the Ascension of Christ II
120

On Pentecost
128

Foreword

THE SAVING WORK OF CHRIST is the second volume in the series *Sermons by Saint Gregory Palamas,* the purpose of which is to bring the life and teaching of this remarkable fourteenth century saint (1296–1359) to a wider readership, to the non-specialist interested in the rich Biblical tradition of the Church Fathers.

Arranged thematically, the work in hand consists of thirteen sermons devoted to the major events in the life of Christ, including two of his most brilliant sermons, "On the Precious and Life-giving Cross" and "On Redemption", Homilies 11 and 16, respectively, in the surviving corpus of sixty-three homilies. The other sermons in this edition, in liturgical sequence and with their corresponding numbers in the corpus, are on Christmas (Homily 58), on the Presentation or Meeting (Homily 5), two sermons on Epiphany or Theophany (Homilies 59 and 60), two sermons on the Transfiguration (Homilies 34 and 35), on Palm Sunday (Homily 15), on the Sabbath and the Lord's Day (Homily 17), two sermons on the the Ascension (Homilies 21 and 22), and on Pentecost (Homily 24).

It was in 1334, while on Mount Athos, in his third year at the hermitage of St. Sabas, which belongs to the Great Lavra, that Palamas experienced a vision in which he was encouraged to share the wisdom bestowed upon him from on high. It seemed that he was carrying a vessel overflowing with milk, which subsequently turned into the finest of wines. The wine emitted such a strong fragrance that it brought great joy to his soul. A youth appeared and rebuked him for not sharing the wine with others and for allowing it to go to waste, for this wine, as he explained, was inexhaustible. The angel then warned Gregory, reminding him of the parable of the talents (*cf.* Matt. 25:14–30). As he later related to his friend and disciple Dorotheus,[1] Palamas understood this vision to mean that the time would come when he would be called upon to transfer his teaching from the simple plane of the ethical (the milk) to the higher plane of the dogmatic word (the wine), which leads heavenward.[2] Thus at the age of about thirty-eight Gregory began to write his Encomium for St. Peter the Athonite, and, at about the same time, he also began to compose what is without doubt the most famous of all his works, Homily 53, "On the Entry of the Mother of God into the Holy of Holies", in which the *Theotokos* is presented as the archetype of the hesychastic way of life, the way of "stillness" (Gk. *hesychia, cf.* Ps. 46:10).

The teaching of St. Gregory and his fellow Hesychasts was based on the understanding that man, the greatest of all God's creatures, had been called to enter into direct and unmediated communion with God even from this present life. The chief manner by which this is achieved is through the grace of God and *noetic* prayer, that is, through the Prayer of the Heart, also known as the Jesus Prayer: *Lord Jesus Christ, Son of God, have mercy upon me.* For the Hesychasts, therefore, true theology, real knowledge of God, is given not to those whose minds have been exercised in lofty concepts *about* God, but to those who, through prayer and ascetic striving in accordance with the commandments of Christ, have been made worthy to behold the vision of Christ in glory, to those who have seen God face to face and share in His very Life.

1. One of the Vlatte brothers (the other being Markos), who built Vlattadon Monastery (1351–1371). Dorotheus later also served as Archbishop of Thessalonica, from 1371 to 1379.

2. Philotheus Kokkinos, *Encomium for our father among the saints, Gregory Palamas, Archbishop of Thessalonica,* ed. J.-P. Migne, *Patrologia Graeca* 151:580A–581B; see esp. crit. ed. Demetrios G. Tsames, *The Hagiological Works of Philotheus Kokkinos, Patriarch of Constantinople,* vol. 1: *Thessalonian Saints,* Center for Byzantine Studies (Thessalonica, 1985), §§ 36–37, pp. 467–468.

Text and Translation

The present work is based on the edition of Panagiotes K. Chrestou.³ The initial translation of the sermons contained in *The Saving Work of Christ* was kindly made available to the editor for correction and improvement by Archimandrite Zacharias of the Holy Monastery of St. John the Baptist, England, and subsequently corrected against the original Greek, oftentimes reworked, and given its present form. Responsibility for the final version of the text, of course, rests entirely with the editor.

I wish to express my deepest gratitude to Abbot Ephraim and the brethren of the Holy Monastery of Vatopedi on Mount Athos for so kindly providing me with a copy of the oldest extant icon of St. Gregory: a 1371 wall-painting from the Chapel of the Holy Unmercenary Physicians (Gk. *Anargyroi*) at Vatopedi (see back cover and p. vi). The front cover icon of the Transfiguration is by Theophan the Greek (*c.* 1330–1410).

A Note on Biblical References

Even though St. Gregory himself used the Septuagint (Greek) text of the Old Testament, for purely practical reasons I have considered it expedient to employ the numbering, names, and wording of the Hebrew (Massoretic) text, as found in the more familiar Authorized (King James) Version. Scriptural quotations have been adjusted in favour of the Septuagint rendering only where significant differences occur. Such instances have been indicated by the use of Lxx.

C. V.

SAINT TIKHON'S ORTHODOX THEOLOGICAL SEMINARY
FEAST *of* THE BIRTH OF THE MOTHER OF GOD
8 SEPTEMBER, 2008

---

3. *Gregory Palamas: The Complete Works*, vols. 9–11, in the series *Greek Fathers of the Church*, nos. 72, 76, and 79 (Thessalonica, 1985–1986), with an accompanying Modern Greek rendering. This is the preliminary text for the critical edition by Professor Vasileios S. Pseutonkas, of the School of Theology in the University of Thessalonica, which is to occupy the sixth and final volume in Chrestou's *Gregory Palamas: Writings* (Thessalonica, 1962ff).

On Christmas

THIS IS THE FESTIVAL of the virgin birth! Our address must be exalted therefore in accordance with the greatness of the feast, and enter into the mystery, as far as this is accessible and permissible, and time allows, that something of its inner power might be revealed even to us. Please strive, brethren, to lift up your minds as well, that they may better perceive the light of divine knowledge, as though brightly illumined by a holy star. For today I see equality of honour between heaven and earth, and a way up for all those below to things above, matching the condescension of those on high. However great the heaven of heavens may be, or the upper waters which form a roof over the celestial regions, or any heavenly place, state or order, they are no more marvellous or honourable than the cave, the manger, the water sprinkled on the infant and His swaddling clothes. For nothing done by God from the beginning of time was more beneficial to all or more divine than Christ's nativity, which we celebrate today.

The pre-eternal and uncircumscribed and almighty Word is now born according to the flesh, without home, without shelter, without dwelling, and placed as a babe in the manger, seen by men's eyes, touched by their hands, and wrapped in layers of swaddling bands. He is not a spiritual creature coming into being after previously not existing; nor flesh which is brought to birth but will soon perish; nor flesh and mind united to form a rational creature, but God and flesh mingled unconfusedly by the divine Mind to form the existence of one theandric hypostasis, who entered the Virgin's womb for a time. By the good pleasure of the Father and the co-operation of the Spirit, the Word who transcends being came into being in this womb and by means of it, and now He is delivered from it and born as an infant, not loosing but preserving the signs of virginity. He is born without suffering, as He was conceived without passion, for as His mother was shown to be above the pleasure of passion when she conceived, so she is above grievous pains when she gives birth. "Before the pain of travail came upon her, she escaped it", as Isaiah says (*cf.* Isa. 66:7 Lxx), and she brought forth in the flesh the pre-eternal Word. Not only is His divinity inscrutable, but the manner in which He was united with flesh is past understanding, His condescension unsurpassable, and the human nature He assumed divinely, ineffably sublime, and so far above all thought and speech, that it does not admit of any comparison with creation. Even though you see in the flesh the child born to the Maid who knew no husband, He is still beyond compare. It says, "He is fair in beauty beside the sons of men" (*cf.* Ps. 45:2 Lxx). It does not say "fairer" but simply "fair", so as not to compare incomparable things: the nature of God Himself to that of mere men.

"God, thy God", it says, "hath anointed thee with the oil of gladness above thy fellows" (Ps. 45:7). The same one is both perfect God and perfect man; the same God is both the one who anoints and is anointed. For it says, "God, thy God hath anointed thee". It is as man that the Word from God the Father is anointed, and He is anointed with the co-eternal Spirit who is of one nature with Him. This is the oil of gladness, which is why, again, it is the same God who is both the divine unction and the one anointed. But although He is anointed as man, as God He has the source of anointing within Himself. That is why he who beheld things in a divine manner saw and foretold that all those anointed by God were partakers of His life. For it is the property of God alone not to partake of the lives of others but to be partaken of, and to have as partakers those who rejoice in the Spirit. Such is the infant born now in the lowly stable, and hymned by us as a babe in the manger.

For He who produced all earthly and heavenly things out of non-being, when He saw that His rational creatures were brought to nothing because of their desire for something greater (*cf.* Gen. 3:5), bestowed upon them Himself, than whom nothing is greater, and to whom nothing is equal or comes near to being equal, and offered Himself to be partaken of by those who so wished, in order that from that time forward we might exercise our desire for something better without risk, although in the beginning we fell into the ultimate danger on that account (*cf.* 1 Cor. 15:26), and in order that each of us, in desiring to become God, might not only be blameless, but also attain to our longing. In a mysterious way, He abolished the pretext for the original fall, which was the superiority and inferiority observable in beings and the resulting envy and treachery, as also the disputes, both open and concealed, which this caused. Because the author of evil did not want to be lower than any of the angels, but to be equal in excellence to the Creator Himself, he was the first to suffer the terrible fall before anyone else. Smitten by envy, he deceitfully attacked Adam and dragged him down to the abyss of Hades by means of the same desire. By so doing, he made Adam's fall difficult to reverse, and it required God's extraordinary presence, which has now been accomplished, to restore him. His own fall, however, he rendered incurable once and for all, because he did not acquire his arrogance from anyone else, but became himself the principle of evil and the fullness of evil, and made himself available to anyone wishing to participate in evil.

Now since it was God's good pleasure to annul the pretext for that pride which brought down His rational creatures, He makes everything like Himself; and because by nature He is equal to Himself and equal in honour, He makes the creation equal to itself by grace and equal in honour. And how was this done? The very Word of God from God emptied Himself in an indescribable way, came down from on high to the lowest state of man's nature, and indissolubly linked it with Himself, and in humbling Himself and becoming poor like us, He raised on high the things below, or rather, He gathered both things into one, mingling humanity with divinity, and by so doing He taught everyone that humility is the road which leads upwards, setting forth today Himself as an example before men and holy angels alike.

Because of this, the angels now possess steadfastness, having learnt in a practical way from the Master that the way to be exalted and to resemble Him is not arrogance but humility. Because of this, men are easily set right, as they recognize humility as the road by which they are recalled. Because of this, the prince of evil, who is conceit itself, has been put to shame and overthrown, whereas previously he imagined that he could somehow stand and was something, inasmuch as he had enslaved some, and pulled them down with himself, through their desire for something greater, while also hoping to do the same to others through their extreme folly. Now he is seen as a plaything, having been well and truly found out by those he had evilly deceived before. Now that Christ has been born, the devil is trampled down by those who were previously under his feet, who are no longer presumptuous, as the destroyer advised, but identify with the lowly (cf. Rom. 12:16), as the Saviour taught through His deeds, and win heavenly exaltation through humility.

That is why God who sits upon the cherubim (Ps. 99:1) is set before us as a babe on earth. He upon whom the six-winged seraphim cannot look, being unable to gaze intently not only at His nature but even at the radiance of His glory, and therefore covering their eyes with their wings (Isa. 6:2), having become flesh, appears to our senses and can be seen by bodily eyes. He who defines all things and is limited by none is contained in a small, makeshift manger. He who holds the universe and grasps it in the hollow of His hand, is wrapped in narrow swaddling bands and fastened into ordinary clothes. He who possesses the riches of inexhaustible treasures submits Himself voluntarily to such great poverty that He does not even have a place at the inn; and so He enters into a cave at the time of His birth, who was brought forth by God timelessly and impassibly and without beginning. And – how great a wonder! – not only does He who shares the nature of the Father on high put on our fallen nature through His birth, nor is He subject merely to the utter poverty of being born in a wretched cave, but right from the very start, while still in the womb, He accepts the final condemnation of our nature. He who is by nature Lord of all is now ranked with the servants and enrolled with them (Luke 2:1-6), clearly making humble service to others no less honourable than the exercise of lordship, or rather, showing the servants as having greater honour than the earthly ruler at that time, provided of course they understood and obeyed the magnificence of grace. For the man who then seemed to rule the world was not counted with the King of heaven, though all his subjects were, nor was this earthly ruler reckoned then as one of them, but the heavenly Lord was.

David, who is a forefather of God on account of Him who has now been born of his line, hymns God somewhere, "Thy hands have made me and fashioned me: give me understanding, that I may learn thy commandments" (Ps. 119:73). What does this mean? That only the Creator can grant true understanding. Anyone who has been vouchsafed understanding and grasped the honour which our nature received from God through being formed by His hands in His own image, will run towards Him, having come to a realization of His love for mankind, and will obey Him and learn His commandments. But how much more so if he comprehends, as far as is possible, this great mystery of our re-creation and restoration. God formed human nature out of the earth with His own hand and breathed His own life into man (Gen. 2:7, cf. 1 Thess. 5:23), whereas everything else He brought into being by His word alone. He then allowed man to be governed by his own thoughts and follow his own initiative, because he was a rational creature with a sovereign will. Left alone, deceived by the evil one's counsel and unable to withstand his assault, man did not keep to what was in accordance with his nature, but slid towards what was unnatural to it. So now God not only forms human nature anew by His own hand in a mysterious way, but also keeps it near Him. Not only does He assume this nature and raise it up from the fall, but He inexpressibly clothes Himself in it and unites Himself inseparably with it and was born as both God and man: from a woman, in the first instance, that He might take upon Himself the same nature which He formed in our forefathers; and from a woman who was a virgin, in the second, so that He might make man new.

If He had been born from seed, He would not have been a new man and, being part of the old stock, and inheriting that fall, He would not have been able to receive the fullness of the incorruptible Godhead in Himself and become an inexhaustible source of hallowing. And so, not only would He not have been able to cleanse, with abundance of power, our forefathers' defilement caused by sin, but neither would He have been sufficient to sanctify those who came later. Just as water stored in a tank would not be sufficient to provide a large city with enough to drink continuously, but would require its own spring, so that it is never surrendered to the enemy on account of thirst; in the same way, neither a man nor a holy angel who, by sharing in grace, had the ability to make things holy, would suffice to sanctify everyone at all times. But creation needed a well containing its own spring, that those who drew near it and drank their full might remain undefeated by the attacks of weaknesses and deprivations inherent in the created world. So neither an angel nor a man, but the Lord Himself came and saved us, being made a man like us for our sake, and continuing unchanged as God. Building now the new Jerusalem, raising up a temple for Himself with living stones (Eph. 2:20–21, cf. 1 Pet. 2:5), and gathering us into a holy and worldwide Church, He sets in its foundation, which is Christ (cf. 1 Cor. 3:11), the ever-flowing fount of grace. For the Lord's eternal fullness of life, the all-wise and omnipotent divine nature, is made one with human nature, which was led astray through lack of counsel, enslaved to the evil one out of weakness, and laid in the deepest caverns of Hades for want of divine life, that the Lord might instil into it wisdom and power and freedom and unfailing life.

And look forthwith at the symbols of this ineffable union and the resulting benefit poured out even upon those far away. A star accompanies the magi (Matt. 2:2–10): coming to a halt when they do, and travelling with them when they move on, or rather, drawing them and inviting them to the road, as their leader escorting them on their journey. It offers itself as their guide when they are on the move, and when they rest awhile it permits them to do so, and itself stays in its place, lest deserting them it should grieve them by its absence, seeming to abandon its rôle as guide before journey's end. For it caused them considerable distress by concealing itself from them when they approached Jerusalem.

Why did it hide from them while they were there? To make them, through their enquiries, unsuspecting heralds of Christ who was born at that time according to the flesh. Because they presumed they would learn from the Jews where Christ was to be born according to the sacred prophecies, the divine star left them, teaching us that we should no longer seek to find out about the law and the prophets from the Jews, but rather to seek after the teaching that comes from heaven, lest we be deprived of grace and the outpouring of light from above. When they left Jerusalem, the star appeared again to their delight, and went before them to lead the way, "till it came and stood over where the young child was" (Matt. 2:9), obviously worshipping with them this earthly and heavenly infant. This star first brings the magi as a birthday gift to God, born upon earth, and through them to the whole Assyrian nation, according to the saying of Isaiah: "In those days the Assyrians shall be the first nation for God, and after them the Egyptians, and Israel shall be the third" (*cf.* Isa. 19:23–24), as is now seen coming to pass. For the veneration by the magi was immediately followed by the flight into Egypt (Matt. 2:13), during which He delivered the Egyptians from idols (*cf.* Isa. 19:1), and after His return from there, a nation worthy of God's possession was chosen from among Israel.

And while Isaiah openly foretold these events, the magi worshipped Him in person, bringing gold and frankincense and myrrh (Matt. 2:11, *cf.* Isa. 60:6) to Him who, through death, symbolized by myrrh, bestows on us divinely inspired life, of which frankincense is an image, and His divine radiance and kingdom, represented by the gold offered to the giver of eternal glory. On account of Him who is born today, shepherds stand in the same choir as angels, sing the same hymn, and strike up a melody together. The angels do not take the shepherds' pipes into their hands, but the shepherds, surrounded by the radiance of the angels' light, find themselves in the midst of the heavenly host and are taught a heavenly song of praise by the angels, or rather a hymn both heavenly and earthly, saying, "Glory to God in the highest, and on earth peace" (Luke 2:14). Now He who dwells on high and reigns over the celestial heights has the earth as His throne, and is glorified on earth as much as there (*cf.* Isa. 66:1, Acts 7:49), by His saints and His angels alike.

But what is the cause of this praise from men and angels together and this much-extolled good news which so gladdens the shepherds and all men? "Behold", it says, "I bring you good tidings of great joy, which shall be to all people" (Luke 2:10). What does this mean, and what is this universal joy? Listen to the Gospel song to the end and you will understand. "Peace", it says, "good will toward men" (Luke 2:14). For God, who was angry with the human race and subjected it to terrible curses, has come in the flesh, granting His peace and reconciling them to the heavenly Father. Behold, says the hymn, He has not been born for us angels, though now that we see Him on earth we extol Him as we do in heaven, but for you men, that is to say, for your sake and in accordance with your nature a Saviour is born, Christ the Lord, in the city of David.

What is meant by linking God's good will with peace? "Peace", it says, "good will toward men". There were times before when He gave signs of peace to men. To Moses "the Lord spake, as a man speaketh unto his friend" (Exod. 33:11); and He found David a man after His own heart (1 Sam. 13:14, Acts 13:22); and He granted tokens of peace to the whole Jewish nation when He came down upon the mountain for their sake and spoke to them through fire and the thick dark cloud (Exod. 19:9, 16–18, Deut. 4:10–11), but not according to His good pleasure. For good will refers to that which is in and of itself well-pleasing, the original and perfect will of God. It was not the original and perfect will of God that He granted benefits, and not even perfect ones, to certain men or to one nation only. That is why, just as God called many people His sons, but there is only one in whom He was well-pleased (*cf.* Matt. 3:17; 17:5), so He gave His peace on many occasions, but only once accompanied by His good pleasure, which He grants, perfect and unchanging, through the incarnation of our Lord Jesus Christ to every race and to as many as desire it.

Brethren, let us preserve this peace in ourselves as far as we can, for we have received it as an inheritance from our Saviour who has now been born, who gives us the Spirit of adoption, through which we have become heirs of God, and joint-heirs with Christ (*cf.* Rom. 8:15, 17). Let us be at peace with God, doing those things which are well-pleasing to Him, living chastely, telling the truth, behaving righteously, "continuing in prayer and supplication" (*cf.* Acts 1:14), "singing and making melody in our heart" (*cf.* Eph. 5:19), not just with our lips. Let us be at peace with ourselves, by subjecting our flesh to our spirit, choosing to conduct ourselves according to our conscience, and having the inner world of our thoughts motivated by good order and purity. Thus we shall put an end to the civil conflict in our own midst. Let us be at peace with one another, "forbearing one another, and forgiving one another, if any man have a quarrel against any: even as Christ forgave you" (Col. 3:13), and showing mercy to each other out of mutual love, just as Christ, solely for love of us, had mercy on us and for our sake came down to us. Then, recalled from the sinful fall through His help and grace, and lifted high above this world by virtues, we may have our citizenship in heavenly places (*cf.* Phil. 3:20), whence also we wait for our hope (*cf.* Rom. 8:23), redemption from corruption and enjoyment of celestial and eternal blessings as children of the heavenly Father.

May we all attain to this, at the future glorious advent and epiphany of our Lord and God and Saviour Jesus Christ, to whom belongs glory unto the ages. Amen.

On the Presentation

BEFORE CHRIST WE ALL SHARED the same ancestral curse and condemnation poured out on all of us from our single forefather, as if it had sprung from the root of the human race and was the common lot of our nature. Each person's individual action attracted either reproof or praise from God, but no one could do anything about the shared curse and condemnation, or the evil inheritance that had been passed down to him and through him would pass to his descendants.

But Christ came, setting human nature free and changing the common curse into a shared blessing. He took upon Himself our guilty nature from the most pure Virgin and united it, new and unmixed with the old seed, to His divine person. He rendered it guiltless and righteous, so that all His spiritual descendants would remain outside the ancestral curse and condemnation. How so? He shares His grace with each one of us as a person, and each receives forgiveness of his sins from Him. For He did not receive from us a human person, but assumed our human nature and renewed it by uniting it with His own person. His wish was to save us all completely and for our sake He bowed the heavens and came down. When by His deeds, words and sufferings He had pointed out all the ways of salvation, He went up to heaven again, drawing after Him those who trusted in Him. His aim was to grant perfect redemption not just to the nature which He had assumed from us in inseparable union, but to each one of those who believed in Him. This He has done and continues to do, reconciling each of us through Himself to the Father, bringing each one back to obedience and thoroughly healing our disobedience.

To this end, He established holy baptism and gave us saving laws. He preached repentance and shared His own body and blood with us. For it is not only human nature in general, but each believer as a person who receives baptism, governs his life by the holy commandments and becomes a partaker of the Bread that makes divine and of the Cup. By these means Christ justified each one of us personally and restored us to obedience to the heavenly Father. He renewed the human nature He took from us and by what He did and suffered in His person united with our nature, He revealed it as sanctified, justified and completely obedient to the Father. Among the things He did and suffered are the events we celebrate today, when He went up, or was taken up, to the ancient Temple for purification, was met by the God-bearing Simeon, and was proclaimed by Anna, who spent her whole life attending to the Temple.

After the Saviour was born of the Virgin and circumcised on the eighth day according to the law, then, as Luke the evangelist says, "when the days of their purification according to the law of Moses were accomplished, they brought him to Jerusalem to present him to the Lord; as it is written in the law of the Lord" (Luke 2:22). He is circumcised according to the law, brought to Jerusalem according to the law, presented to the Lord as it is written in the law and a sacrifice is offered as the law demands.

Notice that the Creator and Lord of the law is completely obedient to the law. What does He achieve by this? He makes our nature obedient in all things to the Father, He completely heals us of its disobedience and transforms the curse on it into a blessing. As all human nature was in Adam, so it is in Christ. All who received their being from the earthly Adam have returned to the earth and been brought down, alas, to Hades. But, according to the apostle, through the heavenly Adam we have all been called up to heaven and made worthy of its glory and grace. Secretly for the present, for it says "your life is hid with Christ in God". But, "when Christ shall appear", at His second manifestation and coming, "then shall ye all appear with him in glory" (Col. 3:3). What does it mean by "all"? All those who have received the adoption of sons in Christ by the Spirit, and have proved by their deeds that they are His spiritual children.

"And when the days of their purification were accomplished they brought him to present him to the Lord" (Luke 2:22). Whose purification? The law says that the parents and the children born from their coming together need to be purified. Also the psalmist says, "I was shapen in iniquity; and in sin did my mother conceive me" (Ps. 51:5). Where there were no parents, only one Virgin Mother, and the child born was conceived without seed, there was of course no need for purification. But this too was an act of obedience which restored disobedient human nature and took away the guilt of its disobedience. So "when the days of their purification were accomplished, they brought him to present him to the Lord", to dedicate Him, to declare openly that He was a firstborn son, as it is written in the law of the Lord, "Every male that openeth the womb shall be called holy to the Lord" (Exod. 13:2, 12, 15; 34:19, Luke 2:23).

He is the only one who opened the womb at His conception, for He was conceived not through parents' coming together but simply through God's salutation and message which the Virgin heard from the angel. So why does the law say "*every* male that openeth the womb"? Just as "prophets" and "anointed ones" are referred to in the plural when God says through the psalmist, "Touch not mine anointed ones, and do my prophets no harm" (Ps. 105:15, 1 Chr. 16:22), even though there is only one anointed and only this one particular prophet, so every firstborn is said to open the womb, even though the only one who truly did so is the holy one of Israel. Then, it says, they brought Him up "to offer a sacrifice according to that which is said in the law of the Lord, A pair of turtledoves, or two young pigeons" (Luke 2:24).

The pair of turtledoves, reflecting the parents' chastity, referred in some way to those yoked together in lawful marriage. The two young pigeons, knowing nothing of marriage, clearly foretold the Virgin and Him who was born of her and was a virgin to the end. Notice how precise the law is. It stipulated a pair of turtledoves which symbolize those yoked in marriage, but was careful not to refer to the young pigeons as a pair, for neither the Mother nor her Son knew anything of the married state. The law prophesied these things and through them foreshadowed the virgin birth, which it declared long before. When the child born in so marvellous a way was brought up to the Temple, the Holy Spirit prepared other, more fitting turtledoves and young pigeons. Who might these be? Simeon and Anna, who could be said to be young pigeons, because of their babe-like innocence of evil, or rightly called turtledoves on account of their utter chastity.

If we run quickly through the Gospel verses, we see that Simeon, a just and devout man, had been warned beforehand by the Holy Spirit and was moved by Him to come unto the Temple at this time. He met the heavenly and earthly infant and took Him in his arms. As God, he offered Him a hymn and a supplication, asking Him to let him depart from the body, declaring Him to all as the light of salvation (*cf.* Luke 2:29–32), and asserting that He was set for the fall of unbelievers and the resurrection of those who believed in Him (*cf.* Luke 2: 34).

Then he conversed with the infant's Virgin Mother. He showed that her grief on account of the child's Cross revealed her as the mother according to nature of the now theandric Babe, and that by disclosing the doubtful thoughts surrounding the child she would dispel them from people's hearts. Simeon gave the true Mother of the paradoxical child clear evidence of her pain at the child's suffering and her intense sorrow and compassion for Him (*cf.* Luke 2:35).

The prophetess Anna, widow of Phanuel, was about eighty-four years old. Devoted to fasts and prayers, she never left the Temple. At that moment, more than ever in the power of the Holy Spirit, she gave thanks to God and announced the good tidings, that redemption, which she declared to be this infant, had come to those who were waiting for it (*cf.* Luke 2:38).

The Holy Spirit sent this dovelike pair into the Temple beforehand to meet Christ when He came, teaching us what sort of people those who receive Christ should be, and what sort of people women who have lost their husbands and men who have lost their wives should be. For this Anna, Phanuel's widow, was both a widow and a prophetess. How was this possible? Because she renounced the worldly cares of everyday life and did not leave the Temple. She spent her days and nights in fasts, vigils, prayers and psalmody, and her life was blameless. So it stands to reason that she recognized the Lord, whom she served by her actions, when He came. As the psalmist and prophet says of Him, "I will sing and I will behave myself wisely in a perfect way. O when wilt thou come unto me?" (Ps. 101:1–2).

Men and women who choose, after being honourably widowed, to draw near to a life of virginity or to live with someone else, should be like this. If you altogether despise second marriages as something base, then hold fast to your purpose and follow in the footsteps of those who stayed unmarried all their lives. At one time Peter had a mother-in-law (*cf.* Mark 1:29–31, Luke 4:38–39), but he did not lag behind the virgin John when they both ran to the tomb where life began (*cf.* John 20:3–6). In some ways he even surpassed John, for he was appointed leader of the leaders by their Lord (*cf.* Matt. 16:18–19, John 21:15–17). When desire is redirected from the flesh to the spirit it raises us to such heights.

Be careful not to stand aloof from marriage as from something vulgar whilst at the same time failing to remain chaste because it is too difficult. In that case, you will drift away and fall unawares, for you are following neither what is according to the law nor what is superior to the law, but what is against the law. We regard widowed people who do not live chastely as worthy of condemnation, and even if they are lawfully joined in a second marriage we do not deem them completely blameless – for Paul says that they have cast off their first faith (*cf.* 1 Tim. 5:11–12, 1 Cor. 7:27, 39–40). So how much more to be condemned are those who prefer illicit pleasure to lawful marriage, and who live with their wives but do not abstain from fornication. It was fornication which brought the universal flood upon those originally called God's sons (Gen. 6:1–7), which caused fire to rain down from heaven on the men of Sodom (Gen. 13:13; 18:20; 19:5–25), and brought defeat and terrible slaughter to the Israelites at the hands of the Moabites (Num. 25:1–9). And at the present time, in my opinion, it brings upon us defeats at our enemies' hands and all sorts of misfortunes and disasters from within and without.

The first to be called sons of God in the Scriptures are the descendants of Enos, who was the first to hope to be called by the Name of the Lord (cf. Gen. 4:26 Lxx). Enos was the son of Seth, whose family was separate from the accursed family of Cain, and lived chastely. For their sake the world continued until, according to the Scripture, they saw the daughters of men, that is, the women of Cain's stock, that they were fair (Gen. 6:2). Overcome by their corrupt beauty, they took wives of all whom they chose, and learnt their ways. Then evil increased on earth and the flood came and swept them all away (Gen. 6:17ff). If on earth in those days Noah and his sons had not been found to be chaste – as shown by the fact that each man had one wife with whom he went into the ark (Gen. 7:13) – there would have been no root or source from which a second world could begin.

Notice that the world would have been destroyed in those days on account of the promiscuous, had it not been preserved for the sake of the chaste. How will people who are unworthy even of this present life, seeing that they pervert its order into disorder, not be banished from the age to come? They will be handed over to the fire of hell because they did not withstand the fire of fleshly pleasures, unless they make haste now to quench it with repentance and wash away with tears the stains it has already caused. They should also be aware that if they do not quickly make a stand against this passion, in time they will be delivered up to worse, shameful, unnatural passions. These are the product of impure desires and attract here and now the fire of hell, which seizes the licentious and carries them away to eternal punishment.

Everyone has heard of the men of Sodom, of their fervour for completely unlawful depravity, the unprecedented rain of fire that fell on them and their destruction. Often a whole town had to bear the consequences of one man's lechery, as in the case of the inhabitants of the town of Shechem who were completely wiped out by Jacob's sons because Shechem defiled Jacob's daughter Dinah (Gen. 34:2–31). If we leave aside now those who lived before the law, the law itself commands that if a bride is found not to be a virgin she is to be stoned (Deut. 22:13–21), and if a priest's daughter plays the harlot she is to be burnt with fire (Lev. 21:9). It is also forbidden to offer the wages of prostitution in the Lord's Temple (Deut. 23:18). When the Israelites defiled themselves with Moabite women, twenty-three thousand men perished by the sword in one day (1 Cor. 10:8, *cf.* Num. 25:1–9, Exod. 32:28). The great Paul tells us, "Neither let us commit fornication, as some of them committed, and fell in one day three and twenty thousand" (1 Cor. 10:8). Such are the penalties for fornication before the law and under the law, once the law was given.

But what about ourselves who have been enjoined to crucify the flesh with the passions and lusts (Gal. 5:24), but fall again into those sins on account of which God's wrath comes upon the children of disobedience (Col. 3:6)? We have been exhorted to mortify our members which are upon the earth, fornication, uncleanness, inordinate affection and lust, and have not heeded the advice (Col. 3:5). At the end of the day, if nothing else, we should at least fear natural disasters: from below, from above, those which have happened already, those eternal ones which threaten us. We should stand in awe of the appearance of Christ, the Sun of righteousness (Mal. 4:2), in the flesh, and walk honestly as in the day (*cf.* Rom. 13:13). We should be afraid of the apostle's warnings, declarations and counsels when he says, "Know ye not that ye are the temple of God and that the Spirit of God dwelleth in you? If any man defile the temple of God, him shall God destroy" (1 Cor. 3:16–17). Also, "Now the works of the flesh are manifest, which are these: fornication, uncleanness, lasciviousness and such like; of the which I tell you before, as I have also told you in time past, that they which do such things shall not inherit the kingdom of God" (Gal. 5:19, 21). Also, "For this ye know, that no whoremonger, nor unclean person, nor covetous man, who is an idolater, hath any inheritance in the kingdom of Christ and of God" (Eph. 5:5).

Also, "This is the will of God, even your sanctification, that ye should abstain from fornication. For God hath not called us to uncleanness, but unto holiness. He therefore that despiseth, despiseth not man, but God, who hath given us his Holy Spirit" (1 Thess. 4:3, 7–8). Who could recount all the sayings of the apostles and prophets on this subject? Those who are chaste, and therefore belong among Christ's members, are commanded by the apostle as follows: "I wrote unto you in an epistle not to company with fornicators" (1 Cor. 5:9). Because they themselves feel no shame, he advises the others to avoid them and awaken shame in them saying, "If any man that is called a brother be a fornicator, with such an one do not eat" (1 Cor. 5:11). Notice that anyone who wallows in fornication is a stain on the whole Church (1 Cor. 5:6), so everyone should turn away from him and drive him out (1 Cor. 5:7). Paul himself delivered to Satan the fornicator in Corinth and neither allowed love to be shown towards him, nor accepted him, until he exhibited fitting repentance (1 Cor. 5:5ff).

Save your soul, O man, from such present and future evils, and from those twofold evils which are both in the present and the future. Esau's descendants were outcasts because he was immoral and sacrilegious (Gen. 25:25ff; 26:34–35, Heb. 12:16). Rehoboam was deprived of most of his kingdom (1 Kgs. 11:43) because his father Solomon, who was exceptionally obsessed with women (1 Kgs. 11:1–4, cf. Neh. 13:26), died without suffering this loss. Solomon was spared on account of David (1 Kgs. 11:34), who with streams of tears and other works of repentance, continuously eroded the curse that at one time was inflicted on him.

The apostle urges us once more, brethren, to flee fornication (1 Cor. 6:18). If Samson had fled from it, he would not have fallen into Delilah's hands after being deprived of the hair of his head and his strength. He would not have been blinded nor lost his life in such an unfortunate way alongside his enemies (Judg. 14:1ff). If they who were led by Moses and to whom he had given the law had fled from fornication they would not have made sacrifices to Baal-peor (Num. 25:3), nor eaten sacrifices of the dead (Num. 25:2–3, and cf. Ps. 106:28, Hosea 9:10), nor fallen as often as they did. If Solomon had fled from it he would not have deserted God who made him king and gave him wisdom, nor would he have erected temples for idols (1 Kgs. 11:2–4).

You will observe that the passion of fornication pushes a person towards ungodliness. Susanna's beauty would not have beguiled the senior judges in Babylon, triumphed over them and resulted in their being stoned, if from the beginning they had fled from defilement and had not watched her every day lasciviously beforehand (Sus. 5–62). The wretched Holofernes would not have died with his neck severed if Judith's sandal had not previously, according to the Scripture, caught his eye and her beauty ensnared his soul (Judith 16:9). Job says, "I made a covenant with mine eyes; why then should I think upon a maid" (Job 31:1), how much less upon a corrupt woman either divorced or married.

Practise the single life as dear to God, or the married life as God's gift. Drink water from your own wells or rather, chastely from your one well. Keep away completely from the adulterated draught, which is the water of the Styx, the stream of the river Acheron. It is full of murderous venom and has poisonous powers, and invariably drags those who drink it down through the trapdoor of hell into its innermost recesses. Flee from the honeyed lips of prostitutes which are skilled in spreading shameful death, namely, separation from God. David said on this subject, "They that wantonly desert thee shall perish" (Ps. 72:27 Lxx).

We, whose bodies have become the temple of God through the Spirit, and in whom the Spirit dwells, must be clean, or at least be cleansed, and remain always undefiled, contenting ourselves with permissible pleasures. We must make haste to attain purity and chastity and avoid fornication and every uncleanness, in order to rejoice throughout all ages with the pure bridegroom in the unsullied bridechambers. By the prayers of the ever-virgin, most pure, all-glorious Mother who bore Him in virginity for our salvation, now and for ever and unto the ages of ages. Amen.

On Epiphany I

REPENTANCE IS THE BEGINNING, middle and end of the Christian way of life, so it is both sought and required before holy baptism, in holy baptism, and after holy baptism. We are asked to express our repentance in words at the time of our baptism, when we are questioned about our good conscience towards God, make a covenant with Him and promise to live a God-pleasing life that bears witness to our love for Him. For, having believed, we promise allegiance to Christ, who is good and surpasses all goodness, renouncing the evil and thoroughly depraved enemy, and we take it upon ourselves to hold with all our strength to God's commandments, which bring about what is good, and to abstain from every evil thought and deed. When asked, we reply, either in person or, as happens in the case of infants being baptized, through our godparents, concerning what we have believed, inwardly accepted and agreed to with our minds. And since, according to the apostle, "With the heart man believeth unto righteousness; and with the mouth confession is made unto salvation" (Rom. 10:10), when we make this good confession with our mouth we receive salvation through the washing of regeneration (Titus 3:5).

As it happens that most people are infants at the time of this divine washing and all that accompanies it, and do not recognize the power of the mystery, come, let us reveal it in a few words in the hearing of all, as the approaching feast demands. For I think that recalling and elucidating rites performed in divine baptism will bring no small benefit, especially to those who listen with understanding. For if through this reminder we discover that we afterwards neglected any of the undertakings made at our baptism, or failed from the very beginning to put certain things into practice, we shall start again by means of repentance.

When the bishop learns that someone has come seeking to be baptized, he first rejoices inwardly, in imitation of the Lord who loves what is good, and gives spiritual thanks to God, who alone wills and brings about every good thing. Then he calls together the church in his care, that together they might celebrate, and assist in the salvation of the person who has come forward. The bishop stands at the sacred altar with the priests and, after openly expressing his thanksgiving with them, he comes out and asks the candidate with what wish he has come to church. When he replies, either himself or through his godparent, if he is an infant, that he desires to become God's, through His mediation and with His help, and to attain to divine blessings, the bishop tells him, "As you are drawing near to God who is true, perfect and sinless, the manner of your approach, your promise and the way you live from now on must be appropriate: that is to say, full of truth and integrity, and blameless". Having given him guidance on living according to the gospel of Christ, he asks again if he chooses to live such a life. Once the candidate has given his agreement, the bishop seals him with the sign of the Cross, and bids the priests to deem his name worthy of being added to the list, placing him from then on among those being saved, as a lover of the life-giving way of life.

Then, having prayed to God once more, the bishop commands that he be stripped of all his clothing and, standing with his face towards the west, that he make gestures with his hands as though he were pushing Satan away, blow at him and renounce him, and upon questioning to make this renunciation three times. The candidate's nakedness signifies putting off the old man (*cf.* Eph. 4:22) and his unholy life; the act of driving someone away with his hands while looking westwards indicates turning away from the darkness of sin; and by blowing he demonstrates that he is breathing out that disposition which is inborn in him because of the former sin, getting rid of it and, as it were, throwing it at the devil as it belongs to him. The threefold declaration of renunciation is the sign of his resolute and perfect escape from God's adversary. Once the person to be baptized has completed these acts, the bishop exhorts him to turn to face the east and, lifting up his hands, to align himself with Christ by responding to three questions. Looking eastwards is a sign that, having fled from evil, he is looking up at the divine light; raising his hands symbolizes prayer with boldness; and the threefold confession when he makes his commitment proves the steadfastness of his promise to God.

Once he has withdrawn in this way from every evil and run with all his strength to the perfection of goodness, the bishop seals him three times with the holy oil of anointing, then lets the priests anoint his whole body. The anointing signifies preparation for holy struggles, and from then on, as the person being baptized sets out in the footsteps of Christ – the first to be martyred under Pontius Pilate – he is put to death with Him, having become dead to sin in mysterious fashion. Holy baptism is a symbol of this death. After the holy unction, he is immediately led to the sacred font, which has been thoroughly sanctified beforehand by various holy rites and ablutions. Once he has been brought, the bishop baptizes him by immersing him three times, invoking at each immersion one of the three persons whom we worship.

Water is a means of cleansing, but not for souls. It can remove dirt from those being baptized, but not the grime that comes from sin. For that reason the Healer of souls, the Father of spirits (Heb. 12:9), Christ, who takes away the sin of the world (John 1:29), enters the water before us to be baptized, as we celebrate today in advance. He draws the grace of the all-holy Spirit from above to dwell in the water with Him, so that later when those being baptized as He was enter the water, He is there, clothing them ineffably with His Spirit, attaching Himself to them, and filling them with the grace that purifies and illumines reasonable spirits. And this is what the divine Paul is referring to: "As many of you as have been baptized into Christ have put on Christ" (Gal. 3:27).

While the three immersions in the water are also the saving invocation of the life-giving Trinity, they represent the Lord's three-day burial. Following this, the person being baptized comes out of the water the same number of times, because otherwise he could not have been submerged three times, but also because this signifies the resurrection from sin of the three parts of the soul, and the return of the mind, soul and body, all three together, to incorruption. Thus in divine baptism both death and life can be seen, the tomb together with the resurrection, just as the Lord, who "in that he died, he died unto sin once: but in that he liveth, he liveth continuously unto God" (cf. Rom. 6:10). And what the Lord had said, that "the prince of this world cometh, and will find nothing in me" (cf. John 14:30), should also apply to us who have been baptized into His death. Having died to sin through divine baptism, we ought to be alive to God through virtue, so that when the prince of darkness comes looking, he may find nothing in us pleasing to him. And as Christ has risen from the dead, "death hath no more dominion over him" (Rom. 6:9), and in the same way we, after being raised from the sinful fall through divine baptism, must strive not to be held fast by sin any longer. "So many of us as were baptized into Jesus Christ were baptized into his death. Therefore we are buried with him by baptism: that like as Christ was raised up from the dead by the glory of the Father, even so we also should walk in newness of life" (Rom. 6:3–4).

For this reason, the bishop, having clothed the person who has been baptized in a radiant white garment, and anointed him with holy chrism, and having made him a communicant of Christ's body and blood, then sends him on his way, showing that he has thenceforth become a child of light, both united in one body with Christ and a partaker of the Holy Spirit. For we are born again (cf. John 3:3–5) and become heavenly sons of God (cf. Rom. 8:14–19, Phil. 2:15, 1 John 3:1–2) instead of earthly beings, eternal instead of transient. God has mystically implanted heavenly grace in our hearts and set the seal of adoption as sons upon us through anointing with this holy chrism, sealing us by means of the all-holy

Spirit for the day of redemption (*cf.* Eph. 4:30), provided we keep this confession firm to the end and fulfil our promise through deeds, though we may renew it through repentance if it drifts a little off course. That is why works of repentance are necessary even after baptism. But if they are absent, the words of our promise to God are not only useless but also condemn us. "Better is it that thou shouldest not vow, than that thou shouldest vow and not pay" (Eccles. 5:5). And, as Peter the leader of the highest company of the apostles says, "It had been better for them not to have known the way of righteousness, than, after they have known it, to turn from the holy commandment delivered unto them. But it is happened unto them according to the true proverb, The dog is turned to his own vomit again; and the sow that was washed to her wallowing in the mire" (2 Pet. 2:21–22). Another of the apostles says, "Shew me thy faith by thy works" (Jas. 2:18), and, "Who is a faithful man? Let him shew his faith by a good manner of life" (*cf.* Jas. 3:13). The Lord Himself asks, "Why call ye me, Lord, Lord, and do not the things which I say?" (Luke 6:46). He is the living and true God, and seeks from us truthful promises, and living, not dead faith: for "faith without works is dead" (Jas. 2:26).

As repentance is the beginning and end of the Christian way of life, the Lord's Forerunner and Baptist, who was himself the starting point of this approach to living, preached saying, "Repent ye: for the kingdom of heaven is at hand" (Matt. 3:2). And the Lord Himself, the perfection of all goodness, said the same in His preaching (Matt. 4:17). Repentance means hating sin and loving virtue, turning away from evil and doing good (*cf.* Ps. 34:14, 1 Pet. 3:11). These acts are preceded, however, by condemning ourselves for our faults, being penitent before God, fleeing to Him for refuge with a contrite heart, and casting ourselves into the ocean of His mercy, considering ourselves unworthy to be counted among His sons. As the prodigal son said when he repented, "Lord, I am not worthy to be called thy son: make me as one of thy hired servants" (*cf.* Luke 15:19).

The Forerunner and Baptist of the Lord publicly raised the subject of the kingdom of heaven, affirming that it was near, so that people might reckon themselves unworthy on account of the greatness of the divine and heavenly kingdom and condemn themselves, which is the beginning of salvation for everyone, and an occasion for returning to God. But he also holds up an axe and states that it is laid at the very root of the tree, all but threatening to fell it (*cf.* Matt. 3:10). Being hewn down is God's sentence on those who justify themselves and sin without repenting, and, in accordance with this decision, once they have been cut off from the present and future life, they are sent away to dark, unquenchable hell-fire. That is why the Baptist, too, warns that after such people have been cut down, inextinguishable fire receives them, making known in this way the awfulness of God's wrath and that eternal punishment, in order to bring to their senses that insensitive race and men like them who came later.

The Lord's Forerunner did not guide men just to the starting point of repentance, which is keeping away from evil things and profitable contrition of heart, but also sought fruits worthy of repentance (Matt. 3:8). What are these? Firstly confession, as practiced by those who came to him at that time. "Then they went out", it says, "and were baptized of him in Jordan, confessing their sins" (Matt. 3:5–6). Next, he looked for righteousness, almsgiving, moderation, love, truthfulness, telling them, "Exact no more than that which is appointed you", "Do violence to no man, neither accuse any falsely" (Luke 3:13, 14), and "He that hath two coats, let him impart to him that hath none; and he that hath meat, let him do likewise" (Luke 3:11). "For every valley shall be filled, and every mountain and hill shall be brought low" (Luke 3:5). What is the hidden meaning of valleys being filled in and mountains being brought low? Exactly what the Lord says plainly, "Every one that exalteth himself shall be abased; and he that humbleth himself shall be exalted" (Luke 18:14). The Baptist also says, "The crooked shall be made straight, and the rough ways shall be made smooth; and all flesh shall see the salvation of God" (Luke 3:5–6). Lying, deceit and slander are crooked, and the rough paths are anger, hatred, envy and remembrance of wrongs, all of which are made straight and level when transformed by the works of repentance. And so "all flesh", that is, every person of every nation and race who straightens and smoothes himself out through repentance, "shall see the salvation of God" (Luke 3:6). As I speak these words to you, brethren, I feel no small pain in my soul, that we who were long ago vouchsafed Christian baptism have not yet accomplished those very things which John demanded of those approaching his own baptism. Yet the Lord's baptism, of which we were deemed worthy, is as far superior to the baptism given by John in those days, as the grace of the Holy Spirit is more excellent than water; and in proof of this the Lord said to His disciples, "John truly baptized with water; but ye shall be baptized with the Holy Ghost" (Acts 1:5). Whereas John baptized so that people would believe in Him who was coming, the Lord transformed John's baptism through Himself, mystically planting within it through Himself the pre-eternal fount of grace. While John was teaching these things and baptizing those who approached, Jesus came from Nazareth in Galilee to the Jordan, to be baptized by John (Matt. 3:13, Mark 1:9, Luke 3:21, *cf.* John 1:29–31). He did not come on the twelfth day after His birth, as we now keep this feast, rightly choosing to commemorate each year everything accomplished in the course of the dispensation whereby God became man. He came rather when He had reached thirty years of age, as Luke relates (Luke 3:23), seeming to be one of the crowd, with no indication that He was at all different, in simplicity and utter lowliness and obscurity.

John, however, knew through the clear vision of the Spirit that He was drawing near, and said to the multitude, "There standeth one among you, whom ye know not, who is after me", according to His birth and appearance in the flesh, but "was before me" (*cf.* John 1:26–27, 15), as God, the Word and Son of God, begotten of the Father before all ages, and now bearing bodily the fullness of the Godhead (Col. 2:9), "the latchet of whose shoes I am not worthy to unloose" (Luke 3:16). What else can the shoes of the Word of God be except, obviously, the flesh, which He put on for our sake? The strap of these shoes is the way in which His divinity is joined with His flesh, which is beyond words, and which even the highest man born of woman (*cf.* Matt. 11:11) is inadequate to analyse and clarify. "He", says John, "shall baptize you with the Holy Ghost, and with fire" (Matt. 3:11); fire, that is to say, which is capable of enlightening and punishing, with each one receiving what is appropriate, according to what his disposition merits. We are all His rational field (1 Cor. 3:9), and He has "the winnowing-fan" for that field "in His hand" (Matt. 3:12), meaning the powers who minister to Him and the angels who will serve Him at the coming Judgment, separating the tares from the wheat (*cf.* Matt. 13:39–42). You should understand His hand to be His power. "And he will purge", it says, "his floor", that is the entire world, "and gather his wheat", those who are fruitful in righteousness, "unto the garner", signifying the heavenly dwellings, "but he will burn up the chaff" as being of no use, meaning those who are barren with regard to virtue, "with unquenchable fire" (Matt. 3:12). If that fire will never be extinguished, it must have inexhaustible fuel, and this shows that damnation is eternal.

John was saying such things as this to the crowds before the Lord came to the Jordan and while He was present. When John saw Him bowing down he himself bent low and "forbad him, saying, I have need to be baptized of thee" (Matt. 3:14), for I was born from the old seed and am an heir of that fall and the defilement it brought, and I myself need cleansing by You. And You, who took flesh from the Holy Virgin without seed, and who alone, as God, are free from sin, You, Lord, come to me? But as a Master giving orders to his servant the Lord says, "Suffer it to be so now" (Matt. 3:15). He added "now", because after the Lord had been baptized that whole place became a spiritual font, and divine grace encompassed John as well as all the others, poured out upon all from that revered body as from a fountain, flowing around all who were worthy, giving divine enlightenment and redeeming them from the ancestral curse.

And this is what John himself said after these things, "This was he of whom I spake, He that cometh after me is preferred before me: for he was before me. And of his fulness have all we received" (John 1:15–16). "Suffer it to be so now", Jesus tells him, "for thus it becometh us", meaning "Me". These words, too, are spoken to John with authority. "Thus it becometh us to fulfil all righteousness" (Matt. 3:15), that is, that I may leave no divine commandment undone, thus perfectly justifying human nature and filling it more visibly with divine and eternal grace. For when I receive baptism at your hands, I shall manifestly draw down upon it from above the Spirit of adoption.

John, hearing the Master's command, "Suffer it to be so", had nothing to say in reply, and let the Lord be baptized. We shall speak tomorrow of what happened next, for these events belong especially to the appointed feastday.

The Spirit comes upon us and departs of His own volition, being of equal might with the Father and the Son. He stays with those who live in repentance, and even if they sin does not leave them, as we have seen from David (2 Sam. 12:1ff, *cf.* Ps. 51:11), but forsakes those who sin without repenting, as we have found out from Saul (*cf.* 1 Sam. 16:14). So may we all, clinging throughout our lives to the works, words and thoughts of repentance, have Him always dwelling within us, to give us understanding, care for us, and grant us heavenly salvation, now and for ever and unto the ages of ages. Amen.

On Epiphany II

YESTERDAY WHEN I WAS IN CHURCH, celebrating with you as you kept the forefeast of the day of Lights, I spoke on such themes as the occasion demanded and said to your charity about Christian baptism, which we have been deemed worthy to receive, that it is both a recognition of God and a promise to God. On the one hand it is faith in, and acknowledgment of, the truth in God; on the other, a covenant and a promise, effected through holy symbols, that our deeds, words and behaviour will be pleasing to God. But we also went on to teach that if we do not put those undertakings into practice, those holy symbols and the verbal promises to God made through them and with them are not only of no benefit, but also rightly bring us under condemnation. Next we expounded the teaching of the Prophet, Forerunner and Baptist John to the crowds, which also deals with the same baptism. Because, as we have said, baptism is the recognition of God, and the Forerunner and Baptist of our Lord and God and Saviour Jesus Christ leads us to recognize Him through his own teaching, showing us that He is pre-eternal and Master of all, Judge of both the living and the dead, who has authority to bring those who are worthy into eternal dwellings, and cast the condemned into hell. And while John bears witness that Christ is also Lord of the angels, he counts himself among the very lowest of His servants.

But because baptism is not just the recognition of God, but also a promise to turn back to Him and to do works that please Him, that is why Christ's Forerunner and Baptist did not merely guide people towards acknowledging Christ, but also preached repentance and sought fruits worthy of repentance: righteousness, almsgiving, moderation, love and the truth. And to make it clear that a promise to God is useless without deeds, and condemns a man, he held out the threat of an axe and drew attention to the unquenchable fire, saying, "Every tree which bringeth not forth good fruit is hewn down, and cast into the fire" (Matt. 3:10). In addition, we explained to your charity the Baptist's words to the Lord Himself when He came to be baptized. Out of reverence, John stepped back and excused himself from performing the deed, asking that he might rather receive baptism from the Lord. We also, however, related what the Lord said to him, giving him orders as a Master does his servant, but at the same time revealing the mystery to him as a friend and relative according to the flesh, and pointing out His good reasons. Speaking to you on that occasion we reached the point where John, having been persuaded, let the Lord be baptized. There remains that part of the Gospel which has now been read in your hearing: "Jesus, when he was baptized, went up straightway out of the water: and, lo, the heavens were opened unto him, and he saw the Spirit of God descending like a dove, and lighting upon him: and lo a voice from heaven, saying, This is my beloved Son, in whom I am well pleased" (Matt. 3:16–17).

Great and exalted, brethren, is the mystery of Christ's baptism contained in these few words. It is both difficult to contemplate and hard to interpret, and no less difficult to comprehend. But since it pertains especially to our salvation, we are persuaded by Him who urges us to search the Scriptures (John 5:39), and take courage to investigate the power of the mystery, as far as it is accessible to us. Just as in the beginning, after God had said, "Let us make man in our image, after our likeness" (Gen. 1:26), when our nature was created in Adam, the life-giving Spirit, who was manifested and given to man by God breathing into him (Gen. 2:7), revealed at once the tri-hypostatic character of the creative divinity to the other creatures, which were brought into existence by the word alone of the Word and made manifest simply by the Father who spoke; so now that our nature was being re-made in Christ, when the Holy Spirit was revealed through His descent from the supracelestial regions upon the Lord being baptized in the Jordan, He disclosed the mystery of the most sublime and all-accomplishing Trinity, which is able to save reasonable creatures.

Why is the mystery of the Holy Trinity shown forth when man is formed and also when he is formed anew? Not just because man is, on earth, the only initiate into this mystery and the only creature to venerate it, but because he alone is in the image of the Trinity. Sensible and irrational animals have only a living spirit, which is incapable of independent existence, and is completely devoid of mind or reason. But the perfectly suprasensible angels and archangels, as they are intelligent and rational, have a mind and reason, but no quickening spirit, since they also lack bodies which would need to be animated by such a spirit. Man is the only creature who, in the image of the tri-hypostatic Being, has a mind, reason, and a spirit which gives life to his body, inasmuch as he also has a body which needs to be infused with life. When our nature was re-made in the Jordan, the most sublime and all-accomplishing Trinity was made manifest, as the archetype of the image in our soul. Therefore those who receive Christian baptism after Christ are baptized with three immersions, whereas John baptized with one immersion in the Jordan. To underline this point, Matthew says, "Jesus, when he was baptized, went up straightway out of the water" (Matt. 3:16).

"And lo", it says, when He had just risen up from under the water, before He had stepped out, "the heavens were opened unto him" (Matt. 3:16). Please make a mental effort, brethren, and focus your minds on what I am saying with the utmost care, that you may understand the power of the mystery of Christian baptism. For Christ's going down into the water and His being underneath it, at the time of His baptism, foreshadowed His descent into Hades;

and, accordingly, His coming up from under the water prefigured His resurrection from the dead.

As a fitting consequence, when He came up from the water the heavens were immediately opened to Him. For at the time of His descent into Hades, He went under the earth for our sake, and on returning thence, He opened all things both to Himself and to us, not just things on or around the earth, but highest heaven itself, to which afterwards He ascended bodily, "whither the forerunner is for us entered" (Heb. 6:20). Just as He foreshowed the saving passion through the mystical bread and cup, and then handed on this mystery to the faithful to perform for their salvation (1 Cor. 11:25, Luke 22:17–20), so He mystically foretold His descent into Hades and His ascent from there through this baptism of His, and afterwards passed on this sacrament to believers to perform that they may be saved. He allowed Himself what was painful and difficult, but bestowed on us communion in His sufferings right from the start through these painless means, causing us, according to the apostle, to be "planted together in the likeness of his death" (Rom. 6:5), that in due time we might also be vouchsafed the promised resurrection.

Having a soul and body like ours, which He assumed from us for our sake, by means of this body He underwent the passion, death and burial for us, and showed forth the resurrection from the tomb that this same body might become immortal. He taught us to accomplish the bloodless sacrifice in remembrance of these events, that through it we might reap salvation. With His soul He went down to Hades and returned, making us all partakers in eternal light and life, and in token of this He handed on to us the practice of holy baptism, that through it we might harvest salvation; and indeed that through each of these two mysteries and through both elements, soul and body, we might be initiated into and receive the seeds of incorruptible life. For our whole salvation depends on these two sacraments, as the entire dispensation whereby God became man is summed up in them.

"The heavens were opened unto him" (Matt. 3:16). It does not say "heaven" but "the heavens were opened unto him", meaning all of them, all the upper realms, lest, when you look up at anything in the sky above us, you might suppose there is something higher and more sublime than He who has now been baptized. Rather you should understand and recognize that there is one nature and dominion, which reaches from the space, infinite as itself, around and above the heavens, to the intermediate regions of the universe and our own furthest bounds, filling everything, leaving nothing outside itself, encompassing and embracing all things for their salvation, and extending beyond them all; and this nature is made known ineffably in three united persons. "The heavens were opened unto him" (Matt. 3:16), that He might be manifestly shown to be the one who existed before the heavens, or rather, who was before anything existed, as being with God, as the Word and Son of God, whose Father was not born before Him, and as having a name with the Father, "Which is above every name" and all speech (Phil. 2:9). For when all those earthly and heavenly things which appeared to be between Him and His Father in heaven were torn asunder and thrown to each side, He alone was shown to be united with the Father and the Spirit, as He existed with Them before anything was made.

"The heavens were opened" (Matt. 3:16), or as Mark says, they were torn. "Coming up out of the water", he says, "he saw the heavens torn open" (Mark 1:10). Why does one evangelist say they were opened, the other, that they were rent apart? That it might not escape those who listen with understanding that the mystery has a twofold character. On the one hand, by saying, "They were opened", the Gospel made it clear that the heavens had been closed to us previously on account of sin and our disobedience to God. For it is written that, after Adam disobeyed God and heard from Him the words, "Dust thou art, and unto dust shalt thou return" (Gen. 3:19), heaven was barred against him (*cf*. Gen. 3:23–24). So it was fitting that the heavens were opened to Christ, who was shown to be obedient in every respect and, as He said to John, fulfilled all righteousness (Matt. 3:15), even through His baptism now.

On the other hand, as the Lord's Forerunner said, "God giveth not the Spirit by measure unto him. The Father loveth the Son, and hath given all things into his hand" (John 3:34–35), and Christ is seen to have received in the flesh all the immeasurable, limitless power and energy of the divine Spirit. The heavens demonstrated in a practical way that all this power and energy cannot be contained in the whole of creation. On that account, when this power was manifested and was, as it were, passing across to the flesh of the divine person, the heavens had not room for it and they split in two. That man spoke well who said to God, "Even heaven is not clean in thy sight" (*cf.* Job 15:15 Lxx). By "heaven" he meant the heavenly angels, archangels, the many-eyed cherubim, the six-winged seraphim, and all the other celestial beings. It is reasonable that not even the heavens, that is to say, the angels there, are pure before the God of heaven, because although they are continuously cleansed and illumined by their participation in the Master's highest hierarchy, they fall short of His absolute purity. Only our human nature, made equal to God in the divine person of Christ, possesses utterly perfect purity and can contain, so to speak, all the radiance and splendour, power and energy of the divine Spirit. When, therefore, the Holy Spirit descended upon Christ in this way, not only were the heavens opened, but the angels themselves drew back.

"And Jesus, when he was baptized went up straightway out of the water: and, lo, the heavens were opened unto him" (Matt. 3:16). Luke, however, says that while Christ was praying, heaven opened. "It came to pass", he says, "that Jesus also being baptized, and praying, the heaven was opened" (Luke 3:21). He was praying while being baptized, while going down into the water and coming up, teaching through His actions that it is not only necessary for the priest performing the sacrament to pray, but the person being initiated must do the same at every sacred rite. If it happens that the priest is more perfect in virtue and sends up more ardent prayers, grace passes through him to the one receiving the sacrament, but if the latter is more worthy and prays with greater zeal, God who wants to have mercy – Oh how inexpressible is His kindness! – does not refuse to give grace through him to the person performing the rite; which is obviously what happened now in the case of John, as he afterwards testified, saying, "Of his fulness have all we received" (John 1:16).

Why did the heavens open only to Jesus when He prayed, and not to anyone else before Him? What do you say? While still an unborn babe John understood the dispensation whereby God became man in the person of the Word of God, and not only leaped for joy with Him in the divine Spirit from his mother's womb, but also passed on grace to his mother (Luke 1:41–45). Once delivered from the womb, he freed his father's mouth from the silence imposed upon it at the command of an angel (Luke 1:19–20, 64). He was a creature of the desert, more exalted than all those born of women (cf. Matt. 11:11), more eminent than all the prophets down the ages (cf. Matt. 11:9, 11). Yet this man was unworthy to unloose the strap of Christ's shoes (Mark 1:7) – whatever that strap might be – so how could someone inferior to him in honour be worthy to open heaven, or rather, what lies above the heavens? That you might realize how very much more exalted than anyone else He is, who is now being baptized in the flesh, consider this. When the Scripture says, "The heavens were opened unto him" (Matt. 3:16), this is shown to us in practice to mean that, not merely the heavens, but the bosom of the heavenly Father was opened to Him. For that is where the Spirit and the voice bearing witness to His true Sonship came from. And the heavens proclaim Him (cf. Ps. 19:1), opening, as it were, mouths as wide as the world, and making quite clear not just to the angels in heaven but to all men on earth that in essence, power and dominion over all, the Son of God is equal in honour to the heavenly Father and to the Spirit who has His origin from the Father by procession.

It was right that the heavens opened only to Christ as He prayed, because, according to the Revelation of John, the sealed book, which may perhaps signify heaven which was previously closed to us, could also not be opened or read by anyone at all in heaven, on earth or under the earth, but, "Only the Lion of the tribe of Judah", it says, "hath prevailed to open it and read it" (cf. Rev. 5:1–5). The patriarch Jacob taught us beforehand who the Lion of the tribe of Judah is, saying, "Judah is a lion's whelp: from this tribe, my son, thou art gone up: reclining thou hast slept as a lion, and as a young lion; who shall rouse him up? A ruler shall not depart from Judah, nor a leader from between his feet, until he comes for whom it is laid up in store, and he is the expectation of the nations" (*cf.* Gen. 49:9–10 Lxx), meaning Christ, who has now manifestly opened all the realms above the heavens, who alone reads the words of providence which have always existed and will exist for ever, the treasures of wisdom hidden in the Father's bosom, and the unsearchable depths and mysteries of the Spirit.

"And Jesus, when he was baptized, went up straightway out of the water: and, lo, the heavens were opened unto him" (Matt. 3:16). Do you see that holy baptism is the gate leading those being baptized into heaven? For it does not just say, "The heavens were opened", but, "were opened unto him". Everything that happened to Him was for our sake. Therefore through Him the heavens opened for us, and they wait for us to enter with their gates flung wide. Stephen, the first among martyrs, bears witness to this before the rest. For when he knelt down and prayed, he gazed upwards and saw what no one had seen before Christ's baptism. "He looked up stedfastly into heaven, and saw the heavens opened, and Jesus in the glory of God" (*cf.* Acts 7:55–56). He not only beheld unspeakable glory and the place beyond the heavens, but also the one He longed for in His Father's glory, and, by means of this glory, Stephen was blessed to be the very first after Christ to look upon things which no one had beheld before Christ, things which even the angelic orders fear to look into (*cf.* 1 Pet. 1:12). Jesus, for whom Stephen yearned, drew him, wanting him to be the first deacon in heaven, much preferred to all the ministering spirits, as he was also the first martyr in the Christian struggle. Through Christ the heavens opened to us, and He cleansed us through Himself, for He needed neither cleansing nor the opening of the heavens.

John saw too, so that he would be able later to say to those who asked, "And I saw, and bare record that this is the Christ, the Son of God" (*cf.* John 1:34). John beheld the Spirit of God descending like a dove and lighting upon Him (John 1:32). The form of the dove testifies to the purity of Him upon whom it descended, for this creature does not fly anywhere dirty or evil-smelling, and therefore joins the Father's voice from above in bearing witness. "And lo", it says, at the same time as the dove's appearance, "a voice from heaven, saying, This is my beloved Son, in whom I am well pleased" (Matt. 3:17): this is He whom My Spirit, by descending and resting upon Him, reveals now as my co-eternal Son. The Father, using His own pre-eternal and consubstantial and supracelestial Spirit as His finger, crying out and pointing from heaven, openly declared and proclaimed to all that the one then being baptized by John in the Jordan was His beloved Son, while at the same time manifesting His unity with Him.

The Spirit did not only appear as the Father's finger pointing to the Son, but came down to Him who was being pointed out by this finger and, as it were, took hold of Him, and also rested upon Him. "John", it says, "bare record, saying, I saw the Spirit descending from heaven like a dove, and it abode upon him" (John 1:32), and not just upon Him but also within Him – as John again bears witness, saying, "Of his fulness have all we received" (John 1:16) – having been in Him invisibly even before the visible descent. The heavenly bodiless angels testify to this, for one of them told the Virgin who conceived Christ, "The Holy Ghost shall come upon thee" (Luke 1:35), and another said to Joseph concerning her, "That which is conceived in her is of the Holy Ghost" (Matt. 1:20). As these events are declared to be not simply a union, but a supernatural, constant and perfect mutual indwelling without confusion, so God too is manifested to us as one God whose almighty divinity is in three hypostases, who reveals Himself to us when and as He graciously wills, as the supracelestial Father, the consubstantial Son and the Holy Spirit who proceeds from the Father and rests in the Son, united without confusion and distinguished without division. There are two who bear witness, and one to whom They bear witness. They testify to Their own divinity, Their shared nature with one another, and to Their distinctness: to Their divinity from the dominion that lies beyond all habitation, by the fact that all the heavens were immediately torn open; to Their shared nature, through Their complete and continuous unity and accord; and to Their distinctness, through the differentiation and relation of the names of the three divine persons.

Because our human nature, assumed by the Son of God, is considered inseparable from Him, it too ascends to such honour that even after He has been made man, there are three divine persons who are worshipped and bring light, and in whom we believe and are baptized, stripping off the old man through divine baptism, and clothing ourselves in Christ, the new Adam. He made our guilty nature new in Himself by taking it upon Himself from the Virgin's blood, as was His good pleasure, and justifying it through Himself. He then freed all those born of Him according to the Spirit from the forefathers' curse and condemnation.

So what shall we say? Since the only-begotten Son of God did not take a human person from us, but our nature, and made it new, being united with it in His own person, does He not impart His grace to each person, and does each of us not receive the forgiveness of sins from Him? How could this be otherwise, as He "will have all men to be perfectly saved" (*cf.* 1 Tim. 2:4), " bowed the heavens and came down" (*cf.* Ps. 18:9) for the sake of all and, having shown us the road to salvation in its entirety through His deeds, words and sufferings, ascended into heaven and drew believers thither? He renewed the nature He received from us for our sake, and showed it to be sanctified and justified, and obedient in all respects to the Father by what He Himself did and suffered being united with it in His person. On the other hand, He has not merely renewed the nature of each of us who believe, but also our person, and granted us remission of sins through divine baptism, through the keeping of His commandments, through the repentance which He bestowed on the fallen, and through the communion of His own body and blood.

And with the Father's words from above concerning Him who was baptized according to the flesh, "This is my beloved Son, in whom I am well pleased" (Matt. 3:17), He made it plain that all those other things spoken earlier through the prophets, the giving of laws, the promises, the granting of sonship, were imperfect, and were neither pronounced nor accomplished in accordance with what God willed beforehand. Rather, they looked towards this present fulfilment, and through what has now been accomplished they too have been brought to perfection. But why refer only to laws, promises, and adoption of sons by the prophets? Even the original foundation of the world looked towards this, towards Him who is baptized below as the Son of man, but testified to from above as God's only beloved Son, for whom and through whom are all things, as the apostle says (cf. Rom. 11:36).

Consequently, man was also brought into being in the beginning because of Him, being formed according to God's image so that one day he might contain his archetype. And the law given by God in paradise was on His account, because God would not have imposed it if it were always to remain unfulfilled. Almost everything said and accomplished subsequently by God was for Him, and you might be right to say that everything in heaven, the orders of angelic beings and the ordinances laid down there, were directed from the start towards this aim, namely, the dispensation whereby God became man, to which they ministered from beginning to end. For God's good pleasure means His good and perfect will preceding the event, and Christ is the only one in whom the Father is well pleased, upon whom He rests and with whom He is perfectly satisfied, "His Wonderful Counsellor, the Angel of His Great Counsel" (cf. Isa. 9:6 LXX), who hears and speaks from His Father, and grants, to those who obey Him, eternal life.

May we all attain to that life, in Christ the King of the ages, to whom belong all glory, honour and worship together with the Father without beginning and the all-holy, good and life-giving Spirit now and for ever and unto the ages of ages. Amen.

On the Transfiguration I

WE ARE FILLED WITH PRAISE AND WONDER when we see this magnificent work of God, the entire visible creation. The pagan Greek sages also extolled and admired it as they investigated it. But whereas we marvel at it to the glory of the Creator, they did so against His glory, for in their wretchedness they worshipped the creature rather than the Creator (*cf.* Rom. 1:25). In the same way, we elucidate the words of the prophets, apostles and fathers for the benefit of those who read them and in honour of the Spirit who spoke through them. The leaders of any given evil heresy also attempt to interpret their writings, but their purpose is to harm their followers and deny that truth which is in accordance with piety, using the words of the Spirit against the Spirit. The words of the gospel of grace are lofty and suitable for mature ears and minds, but these words too our God-bearing Fathers softened in their own mouths, making them appropriate for those of us who are less than perfect, just as mothers devoted to their children chew solid food and render it serviceable and easy to take for babies still at the breast. The moisture in their mothers' mouth is nourishment for the children, and the thoughts in the hearts of our God-bearing Fathers are suitable food for souls that listen and obey. The mouths of evil, disreputable men, however, are full of deadly poison which, when mixed with the words of life, makes even them lethal for careless listeners.

Let us flee from those who reject patristic interpretations and attempt by themselves to deduce the complete opposite. While pretending to concern themselves with the literal sense of the passage, they reject its godly meaning. We should run away from them more than we would from a snake, for when a snake bites it kills the body temporarily, separating it from the immortal soul, but when these evil men get their teeth into a soul they separate it from God, which is eternal death for that soul. Let us escape as far as we can from such people, and take refuge with those who teach piety and salvation in accordance with the traditions of the Fathers.

I have said these things to your charity by way of introduction because today we celebrate the noble feast of Christ's transfiguration, and we shall be addressing the subject of the light that shone on that occasion, which is much opposed even in our own day by the enemies of the light. Let us now briefly set out the words of today's Gospel reading from the beginning to unfold the mystery and demonstrate the truth. "And after six days Jesus taketh Peter, James, and John, and bringeth them up into an high mountain apart, and was transfigured before them: and his face did shine as the sun" (cf. Matt. 17:1–2). The first thing we should consider in this Gospel passage is from what point in time Matthew, Christ's apostle and evangelist, counts the six days preceding the day on which the Lord was transfigured. Six days after which day? Six days after the day when the Lord taught His disciples, saying, "The Son of man shall come in the glory of his Father" (Matt. 16:27), and adding, "There be some standing here, which shall not taste of death, till they see the Son of man coming in his kingdom" (Matt. 16:28). He was referring to the light of His transfiguration as His Father's glory and as His own kingdom. The evangelist Luke indicates the same sequence of events and expresses it more clearly saying, "And it came to pass about an eight days after these sayings, he took Peter and John and James, and went up into a mountain to pray. And as he prayed, the fashion of his countenance was altered, and his raiment was white and glistering" (Luke 9:28–29).

But how do the two accounts agree, when one clearly states that there were eight days between the promise and the manifestation, and the other says it followed after six days? Listen and you will understand. There were eight on the mountain, but they appeared to be six. Three, Peter, James and John, went up with Jesus. There they saw Moses and Elijah with Him, talking to Him, making six. But the Father and the Holy Spirit were invisibly accompanying the Lord. The Father bore witness with His voice that Christ was His beloved Son, and the Holy Spirit joined His brilliance to Christ's in the radiant cloud, and showed that the Son was of one nature with the Father and Himself and united in Their light. For Their wealth consists in Their oneness of nature and in the unified outburst of Their brilliance. So the six persons were eight. Just as there is no contradiction between six and eight in this respect, so there is no disagreement between the evangelists when Matthew says it was after six days, and Luke that it was about eight days after these sayings. It is as if through these two phrases they present us with a figurative allusion to those visibly gathered on the mountain and those mystically present.

Anyone who examines their words closely will see that the evangelists both say the same thing. When Luke mentions eight days, he is not contradicting Matthew's statement that it was after six days, but is including the day on which the words were uttered and the day when the Lord was transfigured. Matthew allows those who read intelligently to understand this, because he says "after" to make it clear that he is referring to the following day, whereas Luke leaves the word out. He does not say, "after eight days", as Matthew says "after six days", but "about eight days passed". So there is no difference in meaning between the evangelists' accounts.

They do, however, indicate another great mystery through this apparent mutual contradiction. Let those of you who are quick witted pay careful heed to what I am going to say. Why did one evangelist say "after six days", whereas the other went beyond a week and mentioned the eighth day? Because the great vision of the light of the Lord's transfiguration is the mystery of the eighth day, that is, of the age to come, which is manifested after this world, which was made in six days, has ceased, and the sixfold action of our senses has been transcended. We have five senses, but if you add speech it brings the number of ways in which our senses work to six. The kingdom of God promised to those who are worthy surpasses not only our senses but also our words. The seventh day is honoured with blessed rest from the activities of our sixfold senses, and after this pause, the kingdom of God shines forth on the eighth day, by virtue of a higher energy. It was this power of the divine Spirit, through which those who are worthy will see God's kingdom, that the Lord foretold, according to the divine Luke, when He declared to His disciples, "There be some of them that stand here, which shall not taste of death, till they have seen the kingdom of God come with power" (Mark 9:1, *cf.* Luke 9:27), bestowing on those who see it the power to behold what is invisible, and purifying them in advance from the deadly, soul-destroying defilement that is sin. The taste of sin is the starting point of evil thoughts, and those who are cleansed beforehand will not experience the death of the soul, having been preserved undefiled in their minds as well, as I understand it, by the power of the manifestation to come.

"There be some of them that stand here, which shall not taste of death, till they have seen the kingdom of God come with power" (Mark 9:1). The King of all is everywhere, and so is His kingdom, so the coming of His kingdom does not mean it arrives here from somewhere else, but that it is revealed through the power of the divine Spirit. That is why He said it would come with power. But this power is not for just anyone, but for those who have stood with the Lord, those who have been established in His faith, men like Peter, James and John, who, as the Scripture tells us, were first brought up a high mountain, that is to say, above the lowliness of our nature. That is why God is imagined to be on a mountain, coming down from His heights and leading us up from the depths of our abasement, that He who cannot be contained might, to an extent compatible with our human nature and our safety, be contained. This idea is not something inferior to man's mind, but far superior and more exalted than it, being instilled in it by the power of the Holy Spirit.

The light of the Lord's transfiguration does not come into being or cease to be, nor is it circumscribed or perceptible to the senses, even though for a short time on the narrow mountain top it was seen by human eyes. Rather, at that moment the initiated disciples of the Lord "passed", as we have been taught, "from flesh to spirit" by the transformation of their senses, which the Spirit wrought in them, and so they saw that ineffable light, when and as much as the Holy Spirit's power granted them to do so. Those who are not aware of this light and who now blaspheme against it think that the chosen apostles saw the light of the Lord's transfiguration with their created faculty of sight, and in this way they endeavour to bring down to the level of a created object not just that light – God's power and kingdom – but even the power of the Holy Spirit, by which divine things are revealed to the worthy. They have not heard, or have not believed, Paul's words, "Eye hath not seen, nor ear heard, neither have entered into the heart of man, the things which God hath prepared for them that love him. But God hath revealed them unto us by His Spirit: for the Spirit searcheth all things, yea, the deep things of God" (1 Cor. 2:9–10).

When the eighth day came, as we have said, the Lord "took Peter and James and John, and went up into a mountain to pray" (*cf.* Luke 9:28). He would always either withdraw from everyone, including the apostles, to pray alone, as when, having fed the five thousand men along with women and children, with five loaves and two fishes, He immediately dismissed them, constrained all the disciples to go into a boat, and went up the mountain to pray (Matt. 14:16–23). Or else He would take a few disciples, those that surpassed the others, with Him. When His saving passion approached He told the other disciples, "Sit ye here, while I go and pray", but took Peter, James and John with Him (Matt. 26:36–37). Here too He took only these three with Him, "and bringeth them up into an high mountain apart, and was transfigured before them" (Matt. 17:1–2), that is to say, while they were watching.

What do the words "and was transfigured" mean? Chrysostom the theologian said that the Lord graciously willed to open up a little of His divinity, and revealed God within Him to the initiated disciples. "As he prayed", says Luke, "the fashion of his countenance was altered" (Luke 9:29), and, as Matthew writes, "His face did shine as the sun" (Matt. 17:2). He compares the light to the sun, not that anyone should imagine that that light was visible to bodily eyes – away with those whose minds are blind and capable of understanding nothing more exalted than visible phenomena! – but that we might know that Christ as God is for those who live by the Spirit and see with spiritual eyes what the sun is for those who live by their senses and see with natural vision. Those who behold God in divine contemplation need no other light, for He alone is the light of those who live for ever. What need is there for a second light when they have the greatest light of all? Thus while He was praying He became radiant and revealed this ineffable light in an indescribable way to the chosen disciples in the presence of the most excellent of the prophets, that He might show us that it is prayer which procures this blessed vision, and we might learn that this brilliance comes about and shines forth when we draw near to God through the virtues, and our minds are united with Him. It is given to all who unceasingly reach up towards God by means of perfect good works and fervent prayer, and is visible to them. Everything about the blessed divine nature is truly beautiful and desirable, and is visible only to those whose minds have been purified. Anyone who gazes at its brilliant rays and its graces, partakes of it to some extent, as though his own face were touched by dazzling light. That is why Moses' countenance was glorified when he spoke with God (Exod. 34:29).

Do you observe that Moses too was transfigured when he went up the mountain and beheld the Lord's glory? But although he underwent transfiguration, he did not bring it about, in accordance with him who said, "the humble light of truth brings me to the point where I see and experience God's radiance". Our Lord Jesus Christ, however, possessed that radiance in His own right. He did not need prayer to illuminate His body with divine light, but He showed how God's splendour would come to the saints and how they would appear. For the righteous shall shine forth as the sun in the kingdom of their Father (Matt. 13:43), and when they have all become divine light, they will behold, as children of that light, Christ's indescribable divine radiance. The glory that proceeds naturally from His divinity was shown on Tabor to be shared by His body as well, because of the unity of His person. Thus His face shone as the sun on account of this light.

There are people in our own times, who boast of pagan Greek learning and the wisdom of this world, and who completely disobey spiritual men in matters of the Spirit, and choose to oppose them. When they hear that the light of the Lord's transfiguration on the mountain was seen by the eyes of the apostles, they immediately reduce it to visible, created light. They drag down that immaterial, never-setting, pre-eternal light, which surpasses not only our senses but also our minds, because they themselves are at a low level, and are incapable of conceiving of anything higher than earthly things. Nevertheless, He who shone with this light proved in advance that it was uncreated by referring to it as the kingdom of God. God's kingdom is not subservient or created, but uniquely unsubduable and invincible. It is beyond the bounds of both time and aeon, and cannot be said to have had a beginning or to have been overtaken by time or age. We believe this kingdom to be the inheritance of those who are being saved.

Given that when He was transfigured the Lord shone and displayed glory, splendour and light, and will come again as He was seen by His disciples on the mountain, does this mean He somehow took this light to Himself, and will have for ever something He did not have before? Perish the blasphemous thought! Because anyone who says so imagines that Christ has three natures: the divine, the human, and the one belonging to this light. It follows that He did not manifest a radiance other than that which He already had invisibly. He possessed the splendour of the divine nature hidden under His flesh. This light, then, is the light of the Godhead, and it is uncreated. According to the theologians, when Christ was transfigured He neither received anything different, nor was changed into anything different, but was revealed to His disciples as He was, opening their eyes and giving sight to the blind. Take note that eyes with natural vision are blind to that light. It is invisible, and those who behold it do so not simply with their bodily eyes, but with eyes transformed by the power of the Holy Spirit.

The apostles were transformed, therefore, and saw that transformation which our human clay had undergone, not at that time, but from the moment in which it had been assumed, when it was deified through union with the Word of God. That is why the Virgin, who mysteriously conceived and bore Him, recognized her child as God incarnate, as did Simeon, when he took Him up in his arms as an infant, and the aged Anna, who came to meet Him (Luke 2:25ff). The power of God shone out visibly as if through thin glass to people who had had the eyes of their hearts purified.

Why does He take the leaders, and them alone, and go up with them? Obviously, to show them something great and mysterious. But how could the vision of ordinary light, visible to those chosen before they ascended, as well as to those left below, be a great mystery? Why would they need strengthening by the Spirit, and why would their eyes have to be assisted and changed by the Spirit to see such light, if it were visible and created? How could ordinary light be the glory and the kingdom of the Father and the Spirit? How could Christ come in that sort of glory and kingdom in the age to come, when there will be no need for air, light, place or anything of the sort, but God, according to the apostle, will be everything for us? (*cf.* 1 Cor. 15:28). Clearly if He will be everything for us, He will also be our light. Again this demonstrates that this light is the light of the Godhead, because John, the greatest theologian among the evangelists, shows in the Revelation that the everlasting future "city had no need of the sun, neither of the moon, to shine in it: for the glory of God did lighten it, and the Lamb is the light thereof" (Rev. 21:23). Surely here he is also pointing us towards Jesus divinely transfigured on Tabor, whose light is His body, and who, instead of daylight, has the glory of divinity as revealed on the mountain to those who came up with Him. Of the inhabitants of that city John says, "They need no candle, neither light: and there shall be no night there" (*cf.* Rev. 22:5). What light is this, in which there is no variableness, nor shadow of turning? (Jas. 1:17). What is this unchangeable and never-setting light? Is it not the divine light?

How could Moses and Elijah, and particularly Moses who was a spirit without a body, have been seen and glorified by means of ordinary light? For they appeared in glory, and spoke of His departure, which He was to accomplish at Jerusalem (Luke 9:31). And how did the apostles recognize men they had never seen before, except by the revealing power of that light?

In order not to strain your understanding too much, we shall keep the remaining verses of the Gospel for the time of the holy and divine Liturgy. We believe what we have been taught by those enlightened by Christ, which they alone know with certainty – "My secrets are for me and those who are mine", as God said through the prophet (Isa. 24:16 Lxx, *cf.* Dan. 2:27ff). So, rightly believing what we were taught, and understanding the mystery of the Lord's transfiguration, let us make our way towards the radiance of that light. As we long for the beauty of unchanging glory, let us cleanse the eyes of our understanding from all earthly defilements, despising every delight and beauty that is not lasting, for sweet as it may be, it procures eternal suffering, and though it may enhance the body, it clothes the soul in that ugly robe of sin, on account of which the man without the garment of incorruptible union was bound and taken away into outer darkness (*cf.* Matt. 22:11–13).

May we all be delivered from such a fate by the illumination and knowledge of the pre-eternal, immaterial light of the Lord's transfiguration, to His glory and the glory of His Father without beginning and the life-giving Spirit, whose radiance, divinity, glory, kingdom and power are one and the same, now and for ever and unto the ages of ages. Amen.

On the Transfiguration II

THE PROPHET ISAIAH FORETOLD in respect of the gospel that, "The Lord will give a concise word on the earth" (*cf.* Isa. 10:23 Lxx). A concise word is an utterance containing an abundance of meaning in a few phrases. So let us look again at the Gospel passage, which we examined earlier, and add what we left out, that we may take our fill of the incorruptible meaning stored up in it, and all receive divine inspiration.

"At that time Jesus taketh Peter, James, and John, and bringeth them up into an high mountain apart, and was transfigured before them: and his face did shine as the sun" (Matt. 17:1–2, *cf.* Mark 9:2–3). "Behold, now is the acceptable time", brethren, "now is the day of salvation" (2 Cor. 6:2, *cf.* Isa. 49:8), a divine, new and eternal day, not measured in hours, never lengthening or shortening, uninterrupted by night. For us it is the day of the Sun of righteousness (Mal. 4:2), with whom is no variableness, neither shadow of turning (Jas. 1:17). That Sun, since the day when, by the good pleasure of the Father and the cooperation of the Holy Spirit, He lovingly shone upon us and led us "out of darkness into his marvellous light" (1 Pet. 2:9), continues without setting to shine upon us for ever.

As the Sun of righteousness (Mal. 4:2) and truth, He does not consent to give light to, or be known perfectly by, those who cultivate lying and either extol injustice or demonstrate it in their deeds. But He shines upon those who act righteously and love truth, is believed by them, and delights them with His rays. Therefore the Scripture says, "Light has dawned for the righteous, and its companion, gladness" (*cf.* Ps. 97:11 Lxx). And the psalmist and prophet also sings to God, "Tabor and Hermon shall rejoice in thy name" (Ps. 89:12), foretelling the joy that those who later saw that illumination would experience. Isaiah tells us "to loose the bands of wickedness, to undo the heavy burdens, and to let the oppressed go free" (Isa. 58:6). What then? "Then shall thy light break forth as the morning, and thine health shall spring forth speedily: and thy righteousness shall go before thee, and the glory of the Lord shall compass thee" (Isa. 58:8 Lxx). Again he says, "If thou take away from the midst of thee the yoke and the stretching forth of the hand, and murmuring speech, and if thou give bread to the hungry from thy heart, and satisfy the afflicted soul; then shall thy light rise in darkness, and thy darkness shall be as noonday" (Isa. 58:9–10 Lxx). For that Sun makes other suns of those upon whom it brightly shines. "Then shall the righteous shine forth as the sun in the kingdom of their Father" (Matt. 13:43).

Let us cast off, brethren, the works of darkness, and let us perform the works of light, that we may not only walk honestly, as in the day (*cf.* Rom. 13:12–13), but also become children of the day (1 Thess. 5:5). And come, let us go up the mountain where Christ shone forth, that we may see what happened there. Or rather, if we become children worthy of that day, the Word of God Himself will take us up when the time comes. Now, I beseech you, strive to lift up the eyes of your understanding towards the light of the gospel message, that you may be transformed by the renewing of your mind (*cf.* Rom. 12:2), and having acquired the divine brightness from above, be conformed to the likeness of the glory of the Lord (*cf.* Rom. 8:29), whose face shone like the sun today on the mountain.

In what way like the sun? There was a time when sunlight was not contained within the disc of the sun, for the light was made first, whereas the Creator of all formed the sun on the fourth day, kindling its light and making it the source of daylight and a luminary to shine by day (Gen. 1:14–19). Similarly, the light of the Godhead was not always contained in Christ's body, for that light existed always without beginning, whereas the human body which the Son of God assumed from us was made later for our sake, receiving the fullness of the Godhead, and so being kindled as a deifying and divinely radiant source of illumination. Christ's face shone like the sun, and His clothes became white as the light. "Shining", says Mark, "exceeding white as snow; so as no fuller on earth can white them" (Mark 9:3).

Both Christ's venerable body and His clothes were radiant with the same light, but not equally so. His face shone like the sun, but His clothes became bright through contact with His body, and in this way He showed us what those robes of glory will be like, which those who are near God will wear in the age to come, and what those garments of sinlessness were like, which Adam took off because of his transgression, appearing naked and ashamed (cf. Gen. 3:10). "The fashion of his countenance was altered, and his raiment was white and glistering", says the divine Luke, regarding everything that happened as beyond comparison (Luke 9:29). Mark, however, describes Christ's clothes as shining exceeding white as snow, but by this comparison he demonstrates that images and illustrations fall short of conveying the appearance of those garments. Snow is indeed white, but it does not shine, because its surface is always uneven, being entirely composed of small bubbles because of the air mixed into it. When a cloud can neither stay whole nor expel the air it holds, it freezes because of the extreme cold, and falls full of air, resembling foam in its whiteness and unevenness.

As snow's whiteness is inadequate to depict how delightful that sight was, the evangelist added the word "shining" to show that the light which made those clothes glistening white was supernatural. It is not a property of light to render the objects it illuminates sparkling and white, but to show up what colour they are. This light, however, apparently revealed, or rather, transformed, the things it shone upon, which visible light cannot do. Even more mysterious is the fact that, even though they were changed, at the same time the light kept them unaltered, as will soon become clear. How could the light with which we are familiar do all this? The evangelist, to indicate that not only the extraordinary radiance and loveliness of the Lord's face was above nature, but also the beauty of His clothes, takes them beyond the bounds of natural beauty by adding the description, "shining" to "white as snow". Then, since skill can also seem to enhance natural beauty, he sets this loveliness above artificial beautification by saying, "so as no fuller on earth can white them" (Mark 9:3).

The pre-eternal Word, who became flesh for our sake, the enhypostatic Wisdom of the Father, also bears within Himself the word of the gospel proclamation. The writing of this message is like a garment, white and clear, but also shining and radiant like pearls, or better put, full of divine worth and inspiration for those who regard the things of the Spirit spiritually, expound the written words in a way worthy of God, and demonstrate that the phrases of the gospel's preaching are such that no fuller on earth, that is to say, none of the wise men of this age, can make them clearer. But why even mention elucidating these words? Such a person cannot even understand them when someone else explains. "The natural man", as the apostle tells us, "receiveth not the things of the Spirit: neither can he know them" (1 Cor. 2:14). As a result he wrongly interprets instances of divine and spiritual radiance, which lie far beyond the reaches of the human mind, as natural light, "intruding into those things which he hath not seen, vainly puffed up by his fleshly mind" (Col. 2:18).

When Peter's understanding had been illuminated by that most blessed sight, he was raised to a greater love and longing for God, and did not want to be separated from that light. "It is good for us to be here", he said to the Lord, "If thou wilt, let us make here three tabernacles; one for thee, and one for Moses, and one for Elias" (Matt. 17:4), not knowing what he was saying (*cf.* Mark 9:6). The time for all things to be restored had not yet come, but even when it does, we shall not need tents made by hand. Nor should the Master be put on the same level as His servants by them all having similar dwellings. As His true Son, Christ is in the bosom of the Father, whereas the prophets, as true sons of Abraham, will dwell, as is fitting, in Abraham's bosom. As Peter spoke these words, without realizing what he was saying, "Behold a bright cloud overshadowed them" (Matt. 17:5), interrupting his words and making clear what sort of tabernacle was appropriate for Christ. But what was this Cloud, and, if it was bright, why did it overshadow them? Was it not the unapproachable light in which God dwells, and with which He covers Himself as with a garment? (Ps. 104:2). "He who maketh the clouds his chariot", as the Scriptures say (Ps. 104:3), and "made darkness his secret place; his pavilion round about him" (Ps. 18:11). And as the apostle says, "He who only hath immortality, dwelling in the light which no man can approach unto" (1 Tim. 6:16). Thus on this occasion the same phenomenon was both light and darkness, overshadowing because of its exceeding brightness.

But the holy theologians bear witness that even the light which was visible earlier to the apostles' eyes was unapproachable. "Today", says one of them, "is the abyss of unapproachable light, today the unlimited outpouring of divine radiance is clearly seen by the apostles on Mount Tabor." And the great Dionysius, having stated that the unapproachable light, in which God is said to dwell, is darkness, says "It is here that everyone found worthy of knowing and seeing God comes". It follows that the light, which the apostles saw shining from the Lord's face, was the same as the bright Cloud, which later overshadowed them. But in the first instance, because it appeared more dimly, it could be seen, whereas later it shone so much more strongly that it was invisible to them on account of its overwhelming brilliance, and thus it overshadowed Christ, the fount of divine, eternal light and the Sun of righteousness (Mal. 4:2). For the one and same light of the visible sun allows us to see by its rays, but also takes away our sight if we look directly at it, since its brilliance exceeds the measure of our eyes.

The visible sun shines as is natural to it; not by its own will, nor only on those it wishes. Christ, however, the Sun of truth and righteousness (*cf.* Mal. 4:2), not only possesses the divine nature with its natural radiance and glory, but also the divine will which is in keeping with these, and He illuminates only those He wishes, and to the extent that He chooses, providentially for their salvation. When He so willed, He shone like the sun and was seen by the apostles' eyes, though not for long. Then when He chose to shine more brilliantly, He was invisible to them on account of His exceeding splendour, as though He had entered a bright Cloud. A voice was heard from the Cloud, saying, "This is my beloved Son, in whom I am well pleased; hear ye him" (Matt. 17:5). After the Lord was baptized in the Jordan the heavens were opened and the same voice came out of that glory (Matt. 3:16–17); that glory which Stephen later saw when, full of the Spirit, the heavens opened to him, and he looked up (Acts 7:55–56). Now this voice is heard out of the Cloud overshadowing Jesus, so this Cloud must be the same as God's celestial glory. How, then, can this heavenly light be a normal, visible light?

The Father's voice from the Cloud taught that all things before the coming of our Lord and God and Saviour Jesus Christ, the sacrifices, the proclamation of laws, the adoption of sons, were imperfect and were neither established nor performed according to the will of God at that time, but were permitted because of the advent and manifestation of the Lord that was to come. He is the beloved Son, in whom God is well pleased (*cf.* Matt. 17:5), upon whom He rests and with whom He is completely satisfied. So He exhorts us to listen to His Son and obey Him. If He says "Enter ye in at the strait gate: for wide is the gate, and broad is the way that leadeth to destruction, and strait is the gate, and narrow is the way, which leadeth unto life", listen to Him (Matt. 7:13–14). And if He tells you that this light is the kingdom of God, hear Him and believe Him, and make yourselves worthy of such a light.

When the bright Cloud appeared and the voice of the Father sounded forth from it, the disciples, it says, fell on their faces (Matt. 17:6). This was not on account of the voice, because the same had happened on many other occasions, not just at the Jordan, but also in Jerusalem when the saving passion was at hand. For the Lord said, "Father, glorify thy name. Then came a voice from heaven, saying, I have both glorified it, and will glorify it again" (John 12:28). The whole multitude heard this, but none of them fell to the ground. But here there was not just a voice, but with the voice limitless light blazed forth. That is why the God-bearing Fathers rightly recognized that the disciples fell on their faces, not because of the voice, but because of that extraordinary supernatural light. As Mark tells us, they were frightened even before the voice came (Mark 9:6), obviously on account of the divine manifestation.

But when, for all these reasons, it clearly appeared that this light is divine, supernatural and uncreated, what befalls those who are excessively taken up with secular, non-spiritual learning, and who are incapable of understanding the things of the Spirit? They fall down a different chasm, for they say that the light is not the divine glory, nor the kingdom of God, His beauty, His grace, or His radiance, as we have been taught by God and the theologians, but affirm instead that what they formerly claimed was visible and created light is God's essence. In the Gospels the Lord tells us that this glory is shared not only by Himself and the Father, but also by the holy angels. As the godly Luke writes, "Whosoever shall be ashamed of me and of my words, of him shall the Son of man be ashamed, when he shall come in his own glory, and in his Father's, and of the holy angels" (Luke 9:26). Consequently, those who assert that this glory is God's essence, say that the essence of both God and the angels is the same, which is the extreme limit of profanity.

Not only angels, but the saints among men are partakers in this glory and the kingdom. But whereas the Father and the Son with the divine Spirit have this glory and kingdom by nature, holy angels and men have them by grace, receiving radiance from that source. The fact that both Moses and Elijah were seen with the Lord in the same glory proves this to us (Matt. 17:3). Nor was it just on Tabor that Moses appeared as a partaker in God's splendour, but also on that occasion when his face was so glorified that the Israelites could not look at it (Exod. 34:29–30, 2 Cor. 3:7). This is demonstrated by the theologian who said that Moses received the Father's immortal glory in his mortal face, and by another who contradicted Eunomius, when the latter said that "the glory of the Almighty was not passed on to the Son", by saying that "even if they were speaking about Moses, he could not tolerate such a statement".

The glory, kingdom and radiance shared by God and His saints are one and the same. That is why the psalmist and prophet sings, "Let the brightness of the Lord our God be upon us" (Ps. 90:17 Lxx). But no one has yet dared to say that God shares one and the same essence with His saints. The one divine splendour is seen now on the mountain to be common to the Word's divinity and His flesh, but that His divinity and flesh have a common essence is an assertion of Eutyches and Dioscorus, not of those who want to be godly. All will see that glory and brightness when the Lord appears, shining from the east to the west (cf. Matt. 24:27), but those who went up with Jesus have seen them already. Nobody, however, has stood in the substance and essence of God (cf. Jer. 23:18 Lxx), and seen or declared His nature. The divine light is given by measure and is received to a greater or lesser extent, being distributed, undividedly divided, according to the worthiness of the recipients. The proof of this is near at hand. Whereas the Lord's face shone more than the sun, His clothes became shining and white as snow. Both Moses and Elijah were seen in this same glory, but neither of them shone like the sun. And the disciples themselves were able to see that light, but not to gaze at it.

Thus is this light measured out and distributed, while remaining entire, and is received more by some, less by others. It is known partly now, partly later, so Paul says, "We know in part, and we prophesy in part" (1 Cor. 13:9). By contrast, God's essence is absolutely indivisible and incomprehensible, and no other being can receive it, either to a greater or lesser extent. Only the accursed Messalians think otherwise, supposing that God's essence can be seen by those among them who are worthy. We, however, turn aside from heretics of earlier ages and our own and believe, as we were taught, that the divine kingdom, glory, splendour, ineffable light, and divine grace can be seen and shared by the saints, but not God's essence. So let us make our way towards the radiance of the light of grace, that we may acknowledge and venerate the threefold Godhead, who shines with a single indescribable radiance from one nature in three persons. Let us lift up the eyes of our understanding to the Word who now sits, with His body, above the vaults of heaven. And He who sits in divine splendour on the right hand of majesty, utters these words to us as if from afar, "If anyone wants to stand in the presence of this glory, let him imitate Me as far as he can, and follow the way and the manner of life I taught on earth".

Let us look with our inner eyes at this great spectacle, our nature, which dwells for all eternity with the immaterial fire of the divinity. And let us take off the coats of skins (*cf.* Gen. 3:21), the earthy and carnal ways of thinking, in which we were clothed because of our transgression, and stand on holy ground (*cf.* Exod. 3:5), each one of us hallowing our own ground by means of virtue and reaching up to God. In this way we shall have boldness when God comes in light, and as we run to Him we shall be enlightened, and, once illumined, shall live for ever to the glory of the one brightness in three Suns, now and for ever and unto the ages of ages. Amen.

On Palm Sunday

"IN AN ACCEPTABLE TIME have I heard thee, and in a day of salvation have I helped thee", said God through Isaiah (Isa. 49:8). It is good today to speak these words of the apostle to your charity: "Behold, now is the accepted time; behold now is the day of salvation" (2 Cor. 6:2). "Let us therefore cast off the works of darkness, and let us work the works of light. Let us walk honestly as in the day" (Rom. 13:12–13). The commemoration of Christ's saving passion is at hand, and the new, great spiritual Passover, which is the reward for dispassion and the prelude of the world to come. Lazarus proclaims it in advance by coming back from the depths of Hades and rising from the dead on the fourth day just by the voice and command of God, who has power over life and death (John 11:1–45). By the inspiration of the Holy Spirit, children and simple people sing praises in advance to the Redeemer from death, who brings souls up from Hades and gives souls and bodies eternal life.

"What man is he that desireth life and to see good days? Keep thy tongue from evil, and thy lips that they speak no guile: depart from evil and do good" (Ps. 34:12–14, *cf.* 1 Pet. 3:10–11). Evil means gluttony, drunkenness and dissolute living. Evil means love of money, being greedy for gain, and injustice. Evil means vainglory, arrogance and pride. Let everyone turn aside from such vices and do those things which are good. What are they? Self-control, fasting, chastity, righteousness, almsgiving, forbearance, love, humility. That by so doing we may worthily partake of the Lamb of God who was sacrificed for our sake, and so receive the earnest of incorruption, and keep it as an assurance of the inheritance promised to us in heaven. Is it hard to do what is good, and are the virtues more difficult than the vices? That is certainly not how I see it. The drunken, self-indulgent person subjects himself because of this to more sufferings than someone who restrains himself; the licentious person suffers more than someone chaste; someone striving to become rich more than someone who lives in contentment with what he has; the person seeking to surround himself with glory than someone who passes his life in obscurity. Since, however, the virtues seem more difficult to us because of our love of comfort, let us force ourselves. "The kingdom of heaven suffereth violence", it says, "and the violent take it by force" (Matt. 11:12).

All of us, eminent and lowly, governors and governed, rich and poor, need diligence and attention to drive these evil passions away from our souls, and introduce the whole range of virtues in their stead. Farmers, shoemakers, builders, tailors, weavers and in general all those who earn their living by their own effort and the work of their hands, provided they throw out of their souls the desire for riches, glory and pleasure, are truly blessed. These are the poor to whom the kingdom of heaven belongs. It was on their account that the Lord said, "Blessed are the poor in spirit" (Matt. 5:3). The poor in spirit are those whose spirits, or souls, are free from boasting, love of glory and fondness for pleasure, and therefore either choose to be poor in external things as well or else courageously bear involuntary poverty. Those who are rich and comfortable, and enjoy fleeting glory, and in general all who long to be like them, will yield to more harmful passions and fall into other worse traps of the devil, which are more difficult to deal with. When someone becomes rich, he does not lay aside his desire for riches, but increases it, grasping at more than he did before. In the same way, pleasure lovers, power seekers, the dissolute and the debauched increase their desires rather than renouncing them.

Rulers and eminent men increase their power so as to commit greater injustices and sin.

That is why it is difficult for a ruler to be saved or for a rich man to enter the kingdom of heaven. "How can ye believe", it says, "which receive honour one of another, and seek not the honour that cometh from God only?" (John 5:44). But if any of you are well off, or eminent or rulers, do not be dismayed. You can, if you wish, seek the glory of God and exert force on yourselves to stop the impetus towards becoming worse, to practise great virtues and to drive away great evils, not just from yourselves, but from many other people, even against their will. Not only can you act honestly and chastely yourselves, but there are many ways in which you can prevent those who want to be unjust and licentious from doing so. Not only can you show yourselves obedient to Christ's Gospel and His teachings, but you can also bring those who are minded to disobey into subjection to Christ's Church and its leaders according to Christ. This you are able to do, not just by means of the power and authority allotted to you by God, but by becoming an example of all that is good to those below you. For subjects become like their rulers.

Everyone needs diligence, force and attention, but not to the same extent. Those exalted in honour, wealth and power, and those who concern themselves with words and the acquisition of wisdom by means of them, even if they wish to be saved, are in need of greater force and diligence, since they are less obedient by nature. Exactly this can be clearly seen in the readings from Christ's Gospel yesterday and today. The miracle performed on Lazarus openly proved the one who did it to be God. But whereas the people were convinced and believed, the rulers at that time, that is to say, the scribes and Pharisees, were so far from being persuaded that they raged against Him even more, and resolved in their madness to hand Him over to death, although everything He had said and done plainly declared Him to be the Lord of life and death. No one can say that the fact that the Lord lifted up His eyes at that time and said, "Father, I thank thee that thou hast heard me", was an obstacle to their regarding Him as equal to the Father, since He went on to say, "I knew that thou hearest me always: but because of the people which stand by I said it, that they may believe that thou hast sent me" (John 11:41–42). So that they might know He was God and came from the Father, and also that He did not work miracles in opposition to God, but in accordance with God's purpose, He lifted up His eyes to God in front of everybody and spoke to Him in words which make it clear that He who was speaking on earth was equal to the heavenly Father on high. In the beginning when man was to be formed, there was a Counsel beforehand. So now also, in the case of Lazarus, when a man was to be formed anew, there was a Counsel first. When man was to be created the Father said to the Son, "Let us make man" (Gen. 1:26), the Son listened to the Father, and man was brought into being. Now, by contrast, the Father listened to the Son speaking, and Lazarus was brought to life.

Notice that the Father and the Son are of equal honour and have the same will. The words are in the form of a prayer for the sake of the crowd standing by, but they are not words of prayer but of lordship and absolute authority. "Lazarus, come forth" (John 11:43). And at once the man who had been dead four days stood before Him alive. Did this come about by the command of the life-giver or His prayer? He cried with a loud voice, again on account of the bystanders, since He could have raised him not only by using His normal voice, but just by His will alone. In the same way, He could have done it from afar and with the stone in place. But instead He came to the grave and spoke to those present, who took away the stone and smelt the stench. Then He cried with a loud voice. He raised him in this manner so that by means of their sight (for they saw Him standing at the grave), their sense of smell (for they were aware of the stench of the man four days dead), their sense of touch (for they used their own hands to take away the stone beforehand from the grave, and afterwards to loose the grave-clothes from his body and the napkin from his face), and their hearing (for the Lord's voice reached the ears of all), they all might understand and believe that it was He who called everything from non-being into being, who upheld all things by the word of His power, and who in the beginning by His word alone made everything that exists out of nothing.

The simple people believed Him in every respect, and did not keep their faith quiet, but began to preach His divinity by deeds and words. After the raising of Lazarus on the fourth day, the Lord found an ass, and, when His disciples had made it ready, as the evangelist Matthew tells us (Matt. 21:1–11), He sat upon it and entered Jerusalem, as had been foretold in Zechariah's prophecy: "Do not fear, O daughter of Zion: behold thy king cometh unto thee: he is just and having salvation; lowly, and riding upon an ass, and upon a colt the foal of an ass" (Zech. 9:9, Matt. 21:5). The prophet shows by these words that this king in the prophecy is the only true king of Zion. "Your king", he says, "does not arouse fear in those who see him. Nor is he an oppressor or an evildoer accompanied by shield-bearers and spearmen, trailing behind him a host of foot-soldiers and cavalry, passing his life in greed for gain, demanding taxes and tributes, and unpleasant and harmful labours and services. By contrast, His banner is humility, poverty and lowliness, and He enters mounted upon an ass, without any human pretensions at all. He is the only righteous King who righteously saves. He is meek, and meekness is His distinctive work." The Lord said of Himself, "Learn of me; for I am meek and lowly in heart" (Matt. 11:29).

So the King who had raised Lazarus from the dead entered Jerusalem sitting upon an ass. Everyone, children, men, old people, immediately spread their garments in the way. They took palm-branches, which are symbols of victory, and went to meet Him as the life-giver and victor over death. They fell at His feet and escorted Him in procession, singing together, not just outside but also inside the precincts of the Temple, "Hosanna to the Son of David, Hosanna in the highest" (Matt. 21:9). "Hosanna" is a song of praise directed to God, which means, "Save us". The additional words "in the highest" show that He is not only praised on earth, nor only by men, but also by the heavenly angels on high.

The people not only sang His praises and called Him God, but they subsequently opposed the scribes and Pharisees' evil purpose against God and their murderous allegations. For the latter were mad enough to say of Him, "This man is not of God, and since he doeth many miracles, if we let him thus alone and do not put him to death, all men will believe on him: and the Romans shall come and take away both our place and nation" (*cf.* John 9:16, 11:47–48). But what did the people say? "Blessed is he that cometh in the name of the Lord: Blessed be the kingdom of our father David that cometh" (Mark 11:9–10). By saying, "Blessed is he that cometh in the name of the Lord", they showed that He was from God the Father and that He came in the name of the Father. As the Lord said of Himself, "I came in the name of my Father (*cf.* John 5:43) and I proceeded forth and came from God" (John 8:42). On the other hand, by saying, "Blessed be the kingdom of our father David that cometh", they showed that this was the kingdom in which, according to prophecy, the Gentiles too, and indeed the Romans, were to believe. For this king was not just Israel's hope, but also the expectation of the Gentiles, according to Jacob's prophecy: "Binding his foal unto the vine", where "foal" refers to the Jewish people who were subject to Him, "and his ass's colt unto the branch of the vine" (Gen. 49:11). The branch of the vine is the Lord's disciples, for the Lord said to them, "I am the vine, ye are the branches" (John 15:5). By this branch, the Lord binds to Himself His "ass's colt", namely the New Israel of the Gentiles, who become sons of Abraham by grace. If, asked the people, this kingdom in which we have put our faith is the hope of the Gentiles too, why should we fear the Romans?

Those who were childlike in innocence but not in intelligence were inspired by the Holy Spirit to offer up to the Lord a faultlessly perfect hymn, and bore witness that, as God, He had brought Lazarus back to life after he had been dead for four days. When the scribes and Pharisees, on the other hand, "saw the wonderful things that he did, and the children crying in the Temple and saying, Hosanna to the Son of David, they were sore displeased and said unto the Lord, Hearest thou what they say?" (Matt. 21:15–16). In fact, it would have been more appropriate for the Lord to put the same question to them, "Can you not see, or hear or understand?" To refute those who were complaining that

He tolerated songs of praise that were fitting for God alone, He replied, "Yes, I hear those who, invisibly enlightened by Myself, declare such things about me. But if these should hold their peace, the stones would immediately cry out. Have you never read the prophecy that, 'Out of the mouth of babes and sucklings thou hast perfected praise'?" (Ps. 8:2, Matt. 21:16). This was another amazing fact, that simple, uneducated children should speak perfectly of the divinity of God made man for our sake, and that their voices should take up the angelic hymn. At the Lord's birth the angels sang, "Glory to God in the highest and on earth" (Luke 2:14), and now at the time of His entry into Jerusalem the children offered up the same hymn, "Hosanna to the Son of David, Hosanna in the highest" (Matt. 21:9).

Let us all, young and old, rulers and subjects, be childlike in innocence, that God may empower us to make a public show of the trophies, and carry aloft the symbols of victory, not just of victory over the evil passions, but over visible and invisible enemies, and may we find the grace of the word to help in time of need (*cf.* Heb. 4:16). The young colt which the Lord deigned to ride for our sake prefigured, although it was only one, the Gentiles' obedience to Him and we, governors and governed alike, are all Gentiles come from them.

In Christ Jesus there is neither male nor female, nor Greek, nor Jew, but all, according to the holy apostle, are one (Gal. 3:28). In the same way, in Him there is neither ruler nor subject, but by His grace we are all one in faith in Him, and belong to one body, His Church, whose head He is. By the grace of the all-holy Spirit we have all drunk of the one Spirit, and have all received one baptism. We all have one hope and one God, who is above all, and through all, and in us all (Eph. 4:6). So let us love one another. Let us bear with one another, seeing that we are members one of another. As the Lord Himself said, the sign that we are His disciples is love. When He departed from this world, the fatherly inheritance He left us was love, and the last prayer He gave us when He ascended to His Father was about love for one another (John 13:33–35).

Let us strive to attain to this fatherly prayer and let us not lose the inheritance He left us nor the sign He gave us, lest we should also lose our sonship, our blessing and our discipleship. If that happens, we shall fall away from the promised hope and be shut out of the spiritual bridechamber. Before His saving passion, when the Lord entered the earthly Jerusalem, not just the people, but also the true rulers of the Gentiles, the Lord's apostles, spread their garments in His way. In the same manner, let us all, rulers as well as subjects, lay down our natural garments before Him, by making our flesh and its impulses subject to the spirit, that we may be made worthy not only to see and worship Christ's saving passion and holy resurrection, but to enjoy communion with Him. "For if", says the apostle, "we have been planted together in the likeness of his death, we shall be also in the likeness of his resurrection" (Rom. 6:5).

To which may we all attain by the grace and love towards mankind of our Lord and God and Saviour Jesus Christ, to whom belong all glory, honour and worship, together with His Father without beginning and the life-giving Spirit, now and for ever and unto the ages of ages. Amen.

On the Precious and Life-giving Cross

THE CROSS OF CHRIST was mysteriously proclaimed in advance and foreshadowed from generations of old and no one was ever reconciled with God except by the power of the Cross. After our First Parents transgressed against God through the tree in paradise, sin came to life, but we died, submitting, even before physical death, to the death of the soul, its separation from God. After the transgression we lived in sin and according to the flesh. Sin "is not subject to the law of God, neither indeed can be. So then they that are in the flesh cannot please God" (Rom. 8:7–8).

As the apostle says, "The flesh lusteth against the Spirit, and the Spirit against the flesh" (Gal. 5:17). God, however, is Spirit, absolute Goodness and Virtue, and our own spirit is after His image and likeness, although sin has made it good for nothing. So how could anyone at all be spiritually renewed and reconciled with God, unless sin and life according to the flesh had been abolished? The Cross of Christ is this abolition of sin. One of our God-bearing Fathers was asked by an unbeliever if he really believed in Christ crucified. "Yes", he replied, "I believe in Him who crucified sin." God Himself has borne witness that there were many who were His friends before and after the law, when the Cross had not yet been revealed. David, the king and prophet, says, as if there were definitely friends of God in his day, "How precious also are thy friends unto me, O God!" (Ps. 139:17 Lxx). I shall now show you, if you listen attentively for the love of God, how it was that people were called friends of God before the Cross.

Although the man of sin, the son of lawlessness (*cf.* 2 Thess. 2:3), by which I mean Antichrist, has not yet come, the theologian whom Christ loved says, "Even now, Beloved, there is antichrist" (*cf.* 1 John 2:18). In the same way, the Cross existed in the time of our ancestors, even before it was accomplished. The great Paul teaches us absolutely clearly that Antichrist is among us, even though he has not yet come, saying, "His mystery doth already work in you" (*cf.* 2 Thess. 2:7). In exactly the same way Christ's Cross was among our forefathers before it came into being, because its mystery was working in them.

Leaving aside Abel, Seth, Enos, Enoch, Noah, and all those up until Noah who were pleasing to God, and their contemporaries, I shall begin with Abraham, who was called the father of many nations, the Jews' father after the flesh and ours by faith. As I am to start with this spiritual father of ours, his good beginning and God's initial call to him, what were the first words God spoke to him? "Get thee out of thy country, and from thy kindred, unto a land that I will show thee" (Gen. 12:1). This utterance certainly bears within it the mystery of the Cross, for it is exactly what Paul says when he glories in the Cross: "The world is crucified unto me" (Gal. 6:14). When someone has fled his home country or the world without turning back, for him his country according to the flesh and the world have been put to death and ceased to exist, and this is the Cross.

God said to Abraham, before he had fled from his life with ungodly men, "Get thee out of thy country unto a land", not, that I will give thee, but "that I will show thee" (Gen. 12:1), so that through this land another, spiritual land might be shown. What were God's first words to Moses once he had fled from Egypt and ascended the mountain? "Put off thy shoes from off thy feet" (Exod. 3:5). This is another mystery of the Cross which follows appropriately upon the first. "You have come out of Egypt", says God, "you have left the service of Pharaoh, and have despised the fact that you were called the son of Pharaoh's daughter. That world of evil servitude has been dissolved and ceased to exist, as far as you are concerned. Nevertheless you still need something more." What can that be? "To take your shoes from off your feet, to lay aside the coats of skins (cf. Gen. 3:21) with which sin clothed you and in which it is at work, separating you from the holy ground. Take these shoes from your feet", which is to say, "do not live any longer according to the flesh and in sin, but let that life which is opposed to God be abolished and put to death. And let the way of thinking based on the flesh (cf. Rom. 8:6–7), and the law in your members warring against the law of your mind, and bringing you into captivity to the law of sin (Rom. 7:23–8:2), no longer hold sway, nor be active, for it has been put to death by the power of this vision of God." Surely this is the Cross. In the divine Paul's words, the Cross is to have crucified "the flesh with the affections and lusts" (Gal. 5:24).

"Put off", He says, "thy shoes from off thy feet, for the place whereon thou standest is holy ground" (Exod. 3:5). These words to Moses revealed that the earth was to be hallowed through the Cross after the manifestation of our Lord and God and Saviour Jesus Christ. At that time, as he looked at that great spectacle of the burning bush which seemed cool as the dew, Moses foresaw the coming of Christ, which was then in the future. The vision in God of the Cross is a mystery greater than that earlier mystery. The great Paul and our holy Fathers hint that there are two mysteries. For Paul not only says, "The world is crucified unto me", but adds, "and I to the world" (Gal. 6:14). The Fathers, for their part, command us not to hasten to ascend the cross before the Cross, as though there were definitely two words of the Cross and two mysteries.

The first mystery of the Cross is flight from the world, and parting from our relatives according to the flesh, if they are a hindrance to piety and a devout life, and training our body, which Paul tells us is of some value (1 Tim. 4:8). In these ways the world and sin are crucified to us, once we have fled from them. According to the second mystery of the Cross, however, we are crucified to the world and the passions, once they have fled from us. It is not of course possible for them to leave us completely and not be at work in our thoughts, unless we attain to contemplation of God. When, through action, we approach contemplation and cultivate and cleanse our inner man, searching for the divine treasure which we ourselves have hidden, and considering the kingdom of God within us, then it is that we crucify ourselves to the world and the passions. Through meditation of this a certain warmth is born in our heart, which chases away evil thoughts like flies, instills spiritual peace and consolation in our soul, and bestows sanctification on our body. As the psalmist says, "My heart was hot within me, while I was musing the fire burned" (Ps. 39:3). One of our God-bearing Fathers taught us about this, saying, "Strive as hard as you can to ensure that your inner labour is according to God's will, and you will conquer the outward passions." The great Paul, urging us on in the same direction, says, "Walk in the Spirit, and ye shall not fulfil the lusts of the flesh" (Gal. 5:16). Elsewhere he exhorts, "Stand therefore, having your loins girt about with truth" (Eph. 6:14). For the contemplative part of the soul strengthens and supports the part concerned with desires, and chases away fleshly lusts. The great Peter tells us with absolute clarity what the references to the loins and the truth mean. "Wherefore", he says, "gird up the loins of your mind, be sober, and hope to the end for the grace that is to be brought unto you at the revelation of Jesus Christ" (1 Pet. 1:13).

Since it is not possible for the evil passions and the world to leave us completely and not be at work in our thoughts, unless we attain to contemplation of God, inasmuch as such contemplation is also the mystery of the Cross, which crucifies those who are worthy of it to the world. That vision which Moses had of the burning bush not consumed by the fire, was also a mystery of the Cross, greater and more perfect than the mystery in the time of Abraham. Is it then the case that Moses was initiated into the more perfect mystery of the Cross, whereas Abraham was not? That would be unreasonable. In fact, Abraham was not initiated at the time when he was called, but afterwards he was, once, twice, and in fact many times, though we do not have enough time to relate everything now.

I shall remind you of Abraham's most wonderful vision of God, when he clearly saw the one God in three persons, before He had been proclaimed to be such (Gen. 18:1–16 Lxx). "The Lord appeared unto him by the oak of Mamre; and he lifted up his eyes and looked, and lo, three men stood by him: and he ran to meet them." He actually saw the one God who appeared to him as three. "God appeared unto him", it says, "and, lo, three men." Having run to meet the three men, however, he addressed them as one, saying, "My Lord, if now I have found favour in thy sight, pass not away from thy servant." The three then discourse with him as though they were one. "And he said to Abraham, Where is Sarah thy wife? I will certainly return unto thee about this same time of year: and Sarah thy wife shall have a son." As the aged Sarah laughed on hearing this, "the Lord said, Wherefore did Sarah laugh?" Notice that the one God is three hypostases, and the three hypostases are one Lord, for it says, "The Lord said".

This is how the mystery of the Cross worked in Abraham. As for Isaac, he himself prefigured Him who was nailed to the Cross for, like Christ, he was obedient to his father unto death. The ram offered instead of him (Gen. 22:13) clearly foreshadowed the Lamb of God who was led to the slaughter for our sake. Even the thicket in which the ram was caught contained the mystery of the sign of the Cross, for it was called the thicket of "Sabek", meaning the thicket of forgiveness (Gen. 22:13 Lxx), just as the Cross was called the wood of salvation. In Isaac's son, Jacob, the mystery and sign of the Cross were also at work, for he increased his flocks by means of wood and water (Gen. 30:37–43). The wood prefigured the wood of the Cross, and the water, holy baptism, which holds within it the mystery of the Cross. "We were baptized into Christ's death", says the apostle (Rom. 6:3). Christ, too, increased His human flocks by means of wood and water, the Cross and baptism.

When Jacob bowed himself upon the end of his staff and blessed his grandchildren with his hands crossed (Gen. 48:9–20), he brought the sign of the Cross even more clearly to light. Because he was obedient to his forefathers from start to finish, he was beloved and blessed, even though Esau hated him for this. He bore every temptation with courage, and the mystery of the Cross was at work throughout his whole life. That is why God said, "Jacob have I loved, but Esau have I hated" (Rom. 9:13, *cf.* Mal. 1:2-3). Something similar, brethren, happens in our case. When someone obeys his earthly and spiritual fathers in accordance with the apostolic commandment saying, "Children, obey your parents" (Eph. 6:1), he is loved by God as having become in this respect like His beloved Son (Matt. 3:17; 17:5, Mark 1:11; 9:7, Luke 3:22; 9:35, 2 Pet. 1:17). But the disobedient son is hateful to God because he is a stranger to any resemblance to His beloved Son. Solomon the wise man makes it clear that this does not just apply to Jacob and Esau, but to everyone at all times. "An obedient son", he says, "is unto life: but the disobedient is unto destruction" (Prov. 13:1 Lxx).

Surely Jacob, the son of obedience, attained to the greater mystery of the Cross, by which I mean the vision of God through which a person is more perfectly crucified to sin, dies to it and lives to virtue? He actually bears witness himself to his vision and his salvation. "For I have seen God", he says, "face to face, and my soul is saved" (Gen. 32:30 Lxx). Where are the people who still go along with the loathsome prattle of those heretics who have appeared in our day? Let them hear that Jacob saw God's face, and not only did he not lose his life but, as he says himself, he was also saved, even though God said, "There shall no man see me, and live" (Exod. 33:20). Surely there cannot be two Gods, one whose face can be seen by the saints, the other whose face is above vision. Perish the impious thought! The face of God visible at the time of His manifestation to those who are worthy, is His energy and grace. Whereas His face which is never seen is what is sometimes called the nature of God, and is beyond the scope of any manifestation or vision. As it is written, "No one hath stood in the substance and essence of the Lord" (Jer. 23:18 Lxx), and either seen God's nature or made it known. So contemplation in God and the sacred mystery of the Cross do not just drive away evil passions, and the devils who devise them, from the soul, but also heretical doctrines. They refute the advocates of such ideas, and thrust them outside the boundaries of Christ's Holy Church, within which we have the privilege now to celebrate and declare the grace and energy of the Cross among our Fathers in the time before the Cross.

The mystery of the Cross was working in Abraham, whereas his son Isaac himself prefigured the one who was afterwards crucified. In the same way, the mystery of the Cross was at work throughout Jacob's life, while Jacob's son Joseph was himself a type and mystery of the divine and human Word who was later crucified. Joseph was led to the slaughter through jealousy, by his kinsmen according to the flesh, for whose sake his father sent him, just as was later the case with Christ. We should not be surprised, however, that Joseph was not murdered but sold. Isaac was not killed either. These men prefigured the truth that was to come, but were not themselves this truth. We can, however, discern in them the twofold mystery of Christ's twofold nature. Their being led to the slaughter foreshadowed the passion according to the flesh of Him who was the God-man, whereas the fact that they did not suffer foretold the impassible nature of His divinity. It was the same with regard to Jacob and Abraham. Although they were tempted, they were victorious, which is what the Scriptures clearly tell us about Christ. Of these four men who were renowned for their virtue and devoutness in the time before the law, two, Abraham and Jacob, had the mystery of the Cross at work in their lives, whereas the other two, Isaac and Joseph, themselves proclaimed the mystery of the Cross beforehand in a marvellous way.

But what about Moses, who was the first to receive the law from God and to share it with others? He was himself saved by means of wood and water before the law was given, when he was exposed to the Nile's currents, hidden away in an ark (Exod. 2:3–10). And by means of wood and water he saved the people of Israel, revealing the Cross by the wood, holy baptism by water (Exod. 14:15–31). Paul, who had looked upon the mysteries, says openly, "They were all baptized unto Moses in the cloud" (1 Cor. 10:2). He also bears witness that, even before the events concerning the sea and his staff, Moses willingly endured Christ's Cross, "Esteeming", he says, "the reproach of Christ greater riches than the treasures of

Egypt" (Heb. 11:26). For the Cross is the reproach of Christ from the standpoint of foolish men. As Paul himself says of Christ, "He endured the cross, despising the shame" (Heb. 12:2). Far in advance, Moses proclaimed in the clearest possible way the figure and form of the Cross and the salvation this sign would bring. For he stood his staff upright and stretched out his hands above it and, when he had formed himself into the shape of a cross upon his staff, this sight completely routed Amalek (Exod. 17:8–13). Again, by placing the serpent of brass sideways upon a standard, he publicly raised up the sign of the Cross and commanded the Jews who had been bitten by serpents to look upon it as a means of salvation, and so he healed the serpents' bites (Num. 21:4–9).

Time fails me to tell of Joshua and his fellow judges and prophets, or David and his successors who, by the working of the mystery of the Cross within them, dried up rivers (2 Kgs. 19:24, Isa. 37:25), made the sun stand still (Josh. 10:13), raised the cities of the ungodly (Gen. 19:25, 2 Pet. 2:6), became mighty in war, put foreign armies to flight, escaped the edge of the sword, quenched the violence of fire, stopped the mouths of lions, put kings to shame (Hebr. 11:33–34, Judg. 4:6; 13:24, Dan. 6:23; 3:23–25; 49–50), reduced captains of fifty to ashes (2 Kgs. 1:13), raised the dead (1 Kgs. 17:23, 2 Kgs. 4:36), made the heavens stand still with a word (2 Kgs. 20:10–11), then let them go, preventing the clouds from giving rain, then letting them do so. If Paul says that faith has done all these things (Heb. 11:32–40), it is because faith is power unto salvation, and all things are possible for him who believes. Clearly the Cross has this same power for believers. "For the preaching of the Cross", to quote Paul again, "is to them that perish foolishness, but unto us which are being saved it is the power of God" (1 Cor. 1:18).

If we move on from all those who lived before or under the law, the Lord Himself, "for whom are all things, and by whom are all things" (Heb. 2:10), said before the Cross, "He that taketh not his cross, and followeth after me, is not worthy of me" (Matt. 10:38). Notice that even before the Cross was fixed in the ground, it was the Cross which brought salvation. When the Lord spoke openly beforehand of His passion and death on the Cross, Peter could not bear to hear. Knowing the Lord's power, he entreated Him, saying, "Be it far from thee, Lord: this shall not be unto thee" (Matt. 16:22). The Lord reprimanded him because in this respect his thinking was human not divine. And "when he had called the people unto him with his disciples also, he said unto them, Whosoever will come after me, let him deny himself, and take up his cross, and follow me. For whosoever will save his soul shall lose it; but whosoever shall lose his soul for my sake and the gospel's, the same shall save it" (Mark 8:34–35, *cf.* Luke 9:23, Matt. 16:24–25).

He also invited the people together with his disciples, and then announced and proclaimed these great and marvellous thoughts which are obviously from God not from men. This was to make it clear that such things were not demanded solely of his chosen disciples, but of everyone who believes in Him. To follow Christ means to live according to His Gospel and to give proof of every virtue and of true piety. The fact that anyone wishing to follow Him must deny himself and take up his cross means he must not spare himself when the moment comes, but be ready to die a dishonourable death for the sake of virtue and the truth of holy doctrines. Though it be a great and marvellous thing for someone to deny himself and surrender himself to extreme dishonour and death, it is not contrary to reason. When earthly kings go to war, they do not let people follow them who are not prepared to die for them. So it is not surprising that the King of Heaven, who came to live on earth according to His promise, should seek such people as His followers in His attack upon the common enemy of the human race. Earthly kings can neither revive those killed in war, nor reward them fittingly for bearing the brunt of the battle. What could someone who is no longer alive receive from them? But in the Lord there is hope even for those who have died, if their death was in defence of what is sacred. To His followers who were daring in battle the Lord gives the reward of eternal life.

Whereas earthly kings require those who follow them to be prepared to die for them, the Lord gave Himself over to death for our sake and commands us to be ready to die not for His sake, but for ours. To make it clear that it is for our own sake, he adds,

"For whosoever will save his soul shall lose it; but whosoever shall lose his soul for my sake and the gospel's, the same shall save it" (Mark 8:35). What does this mean, that anyone who wants to save it shall lose it, and anyone who loses it shall save it? Man is twofold, consisting of our outward man, the body, and our inward man, the soul. When our outward man gives himself over to death, he loses his soul, being separated from it. But when someone loses his soul for Christ and the Gospel, he clearly saves and gains it, because he has procured for it eternal life in heaven. In the resurrection he will recover it, and by means of it he will become, even in his body I say, just as heavenly and eternal as it is. Anyone, by contrast, who clings to life is not prepared to lose his soul in this way, because he loves this fleeting age and everything to do with it. He will inflict loss on his soul, depriving it of true life, and he will lose it, surrendering it along with himself, alas, to eternal punishment. The all-merciful Lord mourned for such people and indicated how great a disaster was theirs by saying, "For what shall it profit a man, if he shall gain the whole world, and lose his own soul? Or what shall a man give in exchange for his soul?" (Mark 8:36–37). For neither his glory nor any of the other deceptive honours and delights of this present age, chosen by him in preference to a death which brings salvation, will go down with him. How could any of these things be given in exchange for a human soul, which is worth more than the whole world?

Even if a man could gain the whole world, brethren, it would be of no benefit to him because he would have lost his own soul. In reality, each person can only acquire an infinitely small share of this world. What a disaster, then, if someone loses his soul in his efforts to acquire this tiny share, rather than choosing to take up the sign and word of the Cross and to follow the giver of life. Now both the sign which we reverence and the word concerning it are, in fact, the Cross.

As the word and the mystery came before the sign itself, we shall expound them to your charity first. Or rather, Paul expounded them before us, Paul who boasts in the Cross, determined not to know anything, save the Lord Jesus, and Him crucified (*cf.* 1 Cor. 2:2). What does he say? The Cross means crucifying the flesh with its passions and desires (cf. Gal. 5:24). Do you think he is referring only to the passions of sensual pleasure and gluttony? In that case he would not have written to the Corinthians, "Since there is among you strife and divisions are ye not carnal and walk as men?" (1 Cor. 3:3). Consequently, anyone who loves glory or money, or simply wants to impose his own will in his eagerness to prevail, is carnal and walks as men, since such things are the source of divisions. As James, the Lord's brother, says, "From whence come wars and fightings among you? Come they not hence, even of your lusts that war in your members? Ye lust and have not: ye fight and war" (Jas. 4:1–2). Crucifying the flesh with its passions and longings means stopping all activity which is displeasing to God. Although our body may pull us down and exert pressure on us, we must still lift it up urgently to the height of the Cross. What am I trying to say? When the Lord was on earth He lived a life of poverty, and not just lived but preached poverty, saying, "Whosoever he be of you that forsaketh not all that he hath, he cannot be my disciple" (Luke 14:33).

May none of you, brethren, be annoyed when you hear us announcing, in unadulterated form, the good and acceptable and perfect will of God, nor be vexed because you think these precepts are unattainable. Bear in mind, firstly, that the kingdom of heaven is subject to violence, and the violent take it by force (Matt 11:12). Listen to Peter, the leader of Christ's apostles, who says, "Christ also suffered for us, leaving us an example, that we should follow his steps" (1 Pet. 2:21). Then you should consider the fact that when someone really learns how much he owes the Master, and is unable to repay in full, he modestly offers as much as he can and freely chooses to. As for the remaining debt, he humbles himself before the Lord and, attracting His compassion through this humility, he makes up for the shortfall. If someone observes his thought reaching out towards riches and wealth, he must realize that this fleshly thought separates him from Christ crucified within him.

How can you begin to take this thought up to the height of the Cross? Having put your hope in Christ who provides for all creation and nurtures it, keep away from all unjust gains, and do not be too attached even to honest income. Put it to good use and let the poor share in it as much as possible. It is the same with the commandment to deny the body and take up our cross. Although godly people who live according to His will have bodies, they are not too attached to them, but make use of their assistance when necessary. Should they be called upon to do so, they are ready to part with them. If you act in this way in respect of the body's attributes and needs, even if you can do nothing more, this is good and pleasing to God. Do you see the thought of fornication forcefully stirred up within? Be aware that you have not yet crucified yourself. How can this be done? Flee from looking inquisitively at women, from unseemly familiarity with them and inappropriate conversation. Reduce the fuel which feeds this passion by giving up excessive drinking, drunkenness, eating your fill and sleeping too much. To the renunciation of these evils add humblemindedness, and call upon God with a contrite heart for help against this passion. Then you too will say, "I have seen the wicked in great power and filled up like the cedars of Lebanon. I passed him by through self-control and, lo, he was not: I sought him in humble prayer, but his place could not be found in me" (*cf.* Ps. 36:35–36 Lxx).

Are you troubled by the thought of love of glory? When you are in meetings or councils, bring to mind the Lord's advice on this subject in the Gospels. Do not try to appear superior to others when you speak. Practise any virtues you have in secret, looking only to God and seen only by Him, "and thy Father which seeth in secret shall reward thee openly" (Matt. 6:6). If, after cutting off the causes of every one of the passions, the thought of them still inwardly troubles you, do not be afraid. It will procure you crowns, since it annoys you but does not win you over, and is not active. It is a dead movement, conquered by your godly struggle.

Such is the word of the Cross (*cf.* 1 Cor. 1:18). It was and is, therefore, a great and truly divine mystery, not only in the time of the prophets before it was accomplished, but also now after it has been fulfilled. Why is this so? On the face of it, anyone who lowers and humbles himself in all respects seems to be bringing dishonour on himself, anyone who flees carnal pleasures appears to be causing himself toil and grief, and anyone who gives away his possessions looks as though he is making himself poor. But by the power of God this poverty, grief and dishonour give birth to inexhaustible riches, inexpressible delight and eternal glory, both in this world and in the world to come. Paul ranks those who do not believe this, and prove their faith by their actions, with the lost, or with the Greeks. "We preach", he says, "Christ crucified, unto the Jews a stumbling block", because they do not believe in the saving passion, "and unto the Greeks foolishness", as they value transitory things above all else because of their complete disbelief in God's promises, "but unto them that are called, Christ the power of God and the wisdom of God" (1 Cor. 1:23).

This is the wisdom and power of God: to be victorious through weakness, exalted through humility, rich through poverty. Not only the word and the mystery of the Cross are divine and to be reverenced, but so also is its sign. For it is a holy, saving and venerable seal, able to hallow and perfect all the good, marvellous and indescribable things which God has done for the human race. It can take away the curse and condemnation, destroy corruption and death, bestow eternal life and blessing. It is the wood of salvation, the regal sceptre, the divine trophy of victory over visible and invisible enemies, even though the heretics' followers are insanely displeased. They have not attained to the apostle's prayer that "they might be able to comprehend with all the saints what is the breadth, and length, and height, and depth" (Eph. 3:18). They have not understood that the Lord's Cross discloses the entire dispensation of His coming in the flesh, and contains within it the whole mystery of this dispensation. Extending in all directions, it embraces everything above, below, around and between. The heretics abhor the sign of the King of Glory (Ps. 24:7–10), putting forward an excuse, in accordance with which, if they were reasonable, they ought to reverence the Cross along with us. The Lord Himself, when He was going to ascend the Cross, openly referred to it as His lifting up and His glory (John 3:14–15). And He announced that when He came again and manifested Himself, this sign of the Son of man would come with power and great glory (Matt. 24:30).

The heretics say that because Christ died nailed to the Cross, they cannot bear to see the form of the wood on which He was put to death. But where was the handwriting nailed which was drawn up against us because of our disobedience, when our forefather stretched out his hand to the tree? How was it taken out of the way and obliterated, enabling us to return to God's blessing? Where did Christ despoil and drive completely away the principalities and powers of the evil spirits, which had taken a hold on our nature since the time of the tree of disobedience? Where did He triumph over them and put them to shame, so that we could be set free? Where was the middle wall of partition broken down and our enmity towards God abolished and put to death? By what means were we reconciled with God and how did we hear the Good News of peace with Him? Surely it was on the Cross and by means of the Cross. Let those who doubt listen to what the apostle writes to the Ephesians, "For Christ is our peace, who hath broken down the middle wall of partition between us; for to make in himself of twain one new man, so making peace; and that he might reconcile both unto God in one body by the cross, having slain the enmity thereby" (Eph. 2:14–16). To the Colossians he writes, "And you, being dead in your sins and the uncircumcision of your flesh, hath he quickened together with him, having forgiven you all trespasses; blotting out the handwriting of ordinances that was against us, which was contrary to us, and took it out of the way, nailing it to his cross; and having spoiled principalities and powers, he made a show of them openly, triumphing over them in it" (Col. 2:13–15).

Surely we should honour and use this divine trophy of the freedom of the whole human race. Its appearance alone puts the serpent, the originator of evil, to flight, triumphs over him and disgraces him, proclaiming him defeated and crushed. It glorifies and magnifies Christ, and displays His victory to the world. If it were really necessary to disregard the Cross because Christ suffered death on it, then His death too would be neither honourable nor salutary. So how can we have been baptized into His death, as the apostle tells us (Rom. 6:3)? And how can we share in

His resurrection, if we have been planted together in the likeness of His death (Rom. 6:5)? On the other hand, if someone were to reverence the sign of the Cross without the Lord's name written upon it, he could justly be accused of doing something incorrect. Since "at the name of Jesus every knee should bow, of things in heaven, and things in the earth, and things under the earth" (Phil. 2:10), and the Cross bears this venerable name. How very foolish not to bow the knee at Christ's Cross!

Inclining our hearts as well as bending our knees, come, "let us worship", with David the psalmist and prophet, "at the place where His feet stood" (Ps. 132:7 Lxx), where His all-embracing hands were outspread and His life-giving body was stretched out for our sake. As we reverence and greet the Cross with faith, let us draw and keep the abundant sanctification flowing from it. Then, at the sublimely glorious future advent of our Lord and God and Saviour Jesus Christ, as we see Him come in glory, we shall rejoice and skip for joy unceasingly, having attained to a place on His right hand and heard the promised joyful words and blessing, to the glory of the Son of God crucified in the flesh for us.

For to Him belongs all glory, together with His Father without beginning and the all-holy, good and life-giving Spirit, now and for ever and unto the ages of ages. Amen.

On Redemption

THE PRE-ETERNAL, uncircumscribed and almighty Word and omnipotent Son of God could clearly have saved man from mortality and servitude to the devil without Himself becoming man. He upholds all things by the word of His power and everything is subject to His divine authority (*cf.* Heb. 1:3). According to Job, He can do everything and nothing is impossible for Him (*cf.* Job 42:2 Lxx). The strength of a created being cannot withstand the power of the Creator, and nothing is more powerful than the Almighty. But the incarnation of the Word of God was the method of deliverance most in keeping with our nature and weakness, and most appropriate for Him who carried it out, for this method had justice on its side, and God does not act without justice. As the psalmist and prophet says, "God is righteous and loveth righteousness" (*cf.* Ps. 11:7), "and there is no unrighteousness in Him" (Ps. 92:15). Man was justly abandoned by God in the beginning as he had first abandoned God. He had voluntarily approached the originator of evil, obeyed him when he treacherously advised the opposite of what God had commanded, and was justly given over to him. In this way, through the evil one's envy and the good Lord's just consent, death came into the world. Because of the devil's overwhelming evil, death became twofold, for he brought about not just physical but also eternal death.

On Redemption

As we had been justly handed over to the devil's service and subjection to death, it was clearly necessary that the human race's return to freedom and life should be accomplished by God in a just way. Not only had man been surrendered to the envious devil by divine righteousness, but the devil had rejected righteousness and become wrongly enamoured of authority, arbitrary power and, above all, tyranny. He took up arms against justice and used his might against mankind. It pleased God that the devil be overcome first by the justice against which he continuously fought, then afterwards by power, through the resurrection and the future Judgment. Justice before power is the best order of events, and that force should come after justice is the work of a truly divine and good Lord, not of a tyrant.

Whereas he who was a murderer from the beginning (John 8:44) attacked us out of envy and hatred, the author of life acted for our sake out of His overwhelming love for mankind and His goodness. The devil achieved his victory and man's fall unjustly and treacherously, but the Redeemer accomplished the final defeat of the originator of evil and the renewal of His creation with righteousness and wisdom. Earlier God left undone what it was in His power to do, so that He might first do what was fitting. In this way, justice was manifested more clearly, having been favoured by Him whose might is unconquerable. Men had to be taught to demonstrate righteousness in their actions now in the time of this mortal life, so that they might be strengthened to hold it fast when eternity comes.

It was also necessary for the conqueror to be conquered by that nature which he had conquered, and for the cheat to be outwitted. To this end it was necessary and indispensable that a man be made who would be sinless (cf. Job 14:4 Lxx). This was, however, impossible, for as the Scripture says, "No one is without sin, even if his life is one day" (Job 14:5 Lxx), and, "Who can say, I have made my heart clean?" (Prov. 20:9), and, "There is none sinless, but one, that is, God" (cf. Matt. 19:17, Mark 10:18). God the Word was from God, pre-eternally begotten of Him, and in Him – for we cannot even imagine that God was ever without His Word – being one God with Him. (For the sun's brightness is not a different light from the sun, and the sun's ray is not a different sun.) So the only sinless Son and Word of the Father became the Son of man, unchanged as God, blameless as man. Who alone, as Isaiah bore witness beforehand, "did no sin, neither was guile found in his mouth" (1 Pet. 2:22, *cf.* Isa. 53:9). Moreover, He alone had not been shapen in iniquity or conceived in sin, as David declared in the Psalms about himself, or rather about everyone (Ps. 51:5). The impulse of the flesh is involuntary and openly wars against the law of the mind. Even though it is brought into subjection by chaste people, and given reign only for the purpose of having children, it ushers in the original condemnation, being subject to corruption and always bringing forth what will perish. In those who are unaware of the honour which our nature has received from God, and have become like animals, it is a movement full of passion.

God was not only born among men but, according to the prophets, born of a holy Virgin far above all defiled thoughts of the flesh. It was the Holy Spirit's coming upon her, not fleshly desire, that caused the Virgin to conceive, and the conception was preceded by good tidings and faith in God's indwelling, not acceptance and experience of passionate longing. In the complete absence of such desire, the pure Virgin said with prayer and spiritual joy to the angel bringing the good tidings, "Behold the handmaid of the Lord; be it unto me according to thy word" (Luke 1:38). Having conceived she gave birth, and it was as if the Victor over the devil, being both man and God, had drawn to Himself the root of the human race but not its sin (*cf.* Heb. 4:15). For He was the only one neither shapen in iniquity nor conceived in sin (*cf.* Ps. 51:5), that is to say, in the fleshly pleasure, passion and unclean thoughts that belong to our nature defiled by transgression. The point of this was that the nature He assumed should be wholly pure and unsullied, so that He Himself would not need to be purified, but would in His wisdom accept everything for our sake. He was rightly called the new Adam, and remained youthful and strong, never growing old. In and through Himself He was to create the old Adam anew and keep him new for ever, since He is able completely to dispel the process of growing old. Originally God created the first Adam undefiled, and he was new until he voluntarily obeyed the devil. He turned aside after the pleasures of the flesh, underwent the defilement of sin, grew old and fell into what is contrary to nature.

The Lord did not just create man anew with His hand in a wonderful way, but held him near Him. He did not merely restore human nature and raise it up from its fall, but in an indescribable fashion clothed Himself in it and indivisibly united Himself with it. He was born both God and man, born of a woman, that He might restore the human nature created by Him, but born of a virgin, that He might make mankind new. If He had been born from seed, He would not have been a new man, nor the author and giver of new life which never grows old. Nor, if He had been of the old stock, could He have received in Himself the fullness of incorruptible divinity. He could not have made His flesh an inexhaustible source of sanctification, with abundant power to wash away the defilement of our First Parents, and sufficient to sanctify everyone who came after them. That is why the Lord's gracious will was that He Himself, not an angel or a man, should mercifully save us and form us anew, coming as a man completely like us while remaining unchanged as God.

So the only man who had no sins to account for, who was in no way worthy of being abandoned by God, was born of the Virgin. Before He knew evil He chose the good, according to the prophecy (*cf.* Isa. 7:16 Lxx). He lived a completely sinless life. There was nothing in His life which could with justice make Him liable to be abandoned by God, and neither did He desert God by transgressing, like the first Adam. He fulfilled every divine commandment, every divine law, so it was right that He should be free from servitude to the devil. This was how the devil, who had defeated man in the beginning, was defeated by man. He boasted of having overcome human nature made in God's image, and now he was brought down from his arrogance, and man was formed anew after the actual death of his soul. He died this death as soon as he tasted the forbidden tree, and it was of this death that both Adam and Eve were warned of God before their disobedience, for He said, "In the day that thou eatest of the tree, thou shalt surely die" (Gen. 2:17).

We were condemned to physical death after the transgression, when God said to Adam, "Dust thou art, and unto dust shalt thou return" (Gen. 3:19). Physical death is when the soul leaves the body and is separated from it. The death of the soul is when God leaves the soul and is separated from it, although in another way, the soul remains immortal. Once separated from God it becomes more ugly and useless than a dead body, but unlike such a body it does not disintegrate after death since it is not composite.

Even in respect of completely inanimate objects, you can see that it is the simpler ones which are more enduring. When the human soul is separated from the divine energy for good, it is not only smitten with inaction, but starts working against itself, sinking from bad to worse. Eventually, after the wretched soul has lived apart from the body without repenting, it will be handed over, together with the body, to the endless, unbearable bondage of eternal damnation which God has prepared for the devil and his angels (cf. Matt. 25:41). All of them are dead, even if they are still active in evil, which is why they were rightly abandoned by the God of true life. The first to undergo this death was Satan, for God justly deserted him on account of his disobedience (cf. Isa. 14:12, Luke 10:18, Rev. 12:9). Then he took us as his partners, pulling us down into disobedience with himself by his evil counsel. Christ, however, redeemed our nature from this state of death, having demonstrated every kind of obedience through His actions in His human life.

Christ clearly had to make immortal not only the human nature which existed in Him, but the human race, and to guide it towards participating in that true life which in due course procures eternal life for the body as well, just as the soul's state of death in due course brought about the death of the body too. That this plan for salvation should be made manifest, and that Christ's way of life should be put before us to emulate, was highly necessary and beneficial. At one time God appeared visibly before man and the good angels that they might imitate Him. Later, when we had cast ourselves down and fallen away from this vision, God came down to us from on high in His surpassing love for mankind, without in any way giving up His divinity, and by living among us set Himself before us as the pattern of the way back to life.

He was also our teacher, using words to show the path that leads to life, and confirming the words of His teaching with great miracles. In this way human nature was justified, as not being evil in itself, but God was justified as well, as not in any way being the cause and maker of evil. If the Father's co-eternal Word had not been made man, sin would have seemed to be part of human nature, for no man had ever been free from sin. The Creator might have been blamed for not creating good things and not being good Himself, or even for being an unjust judge, as if He had unfairly condemned the man who had made himself liable to condemnation.

God took human nature upon Himself to show that it was so far removed from sin and so cleansed that it could be united with His person and remain eternally undivided from Him. By this act He proclaimed to all that God is both good and just, the Maker of good things who upholds fair judgment. When Satan and the apostate angels with him fell from heaven, those angels who kept their place understood that evil was not in angels by nature. Rather, good was natural for them, and their Creator was the essence of goodness. By the Creator's just judgment Satan had been condemned to eternal darkness, because he had created evil for himself by turning away from good. But when Adam fell by turning aside from good to evil, no one remained who was not inclined to evil, and no one was appointed in his place.

So Christ was declared the new Adam. According to Isaiah, He did no sin in deed or thought, and certainly not in word, neither was any deceit in His mouth (*cf.* 1 Pet. 2:22, Isa. 53:9). He does not say "*from* his mouth" but "*in* his mouth", to indicate that His thoughts too were blameless. As He says elsewhere, before He knew evil He chose the good (*cf.* Isa. 7:16 LXX). In this way God was justified, as we have said, and was manifested as truly good and the Maker of good works, since He became a sinless man, and showed forth in Christ the purity which He had inaugurated in human nature.

When this ineffable dispensation was to be manifested and openly displayed, John, called the Forerunner, was sent by God from the desert. He baptized those who came to him and exhorted them to be ready to believe in the one who was to come, who, He said, would baptize them with the Holy Ghost and with fire, and would be as much greater than him as the Holy Spirit was more excellent than water (Matt. 3:11). John bore witness that the one who was to come was the Master, the Creator of all things and the Lord of angels and of men. All men were His reasonable farmland, and their winnowing fan (*cf.* Matt. 3:12), meaning the powers that minister to them, was in His hand and under His authority. Not only did the Lord's Forerunner bear witness to what the one to come would be, but he showed too that Isaiah had foretold He would be the Lord, and that he, John, had been sent as a minister to proclaim His advent and to urge believers to receive Him, saying, "I am the voice of one crying in the wilderness" (John 1:23, *cf.* Isa. 40:3).

The Forerunner bore witness that the Lord existed before He was conceived and born. "He is preferred before me", he said, "for He was before me" (John 1:15), although He was conceived and born after John. If the Lord was sent before John, it was not according to the flesh but obviously before He took flesh. The Forerunner went on to bear witness that the Lord was the Lamb of God who was taking away the sin of the world (John 1:29), thus proclaiming in advance His sacrifice and slaughter for the forgiveness of our sins (*cf.* 1 John 2:2). He testified that He was the Most High who had come down from heaven and was infinitely powerful, for He had not received the Spirit by measure from the Father (John 3:34). To those who believed in Him he promised eternal life and those who did not believe he threatened with God's inescapable wrath (John 3:36). When John's own disciples asked him about the Lord he replied, "He must increase, but I must decrease" (John 3:30). To demonstrate why not only he himself but absolutely everything as far below the Lord as the earth was lower than the heavens, he said, "He that cometh from above is above all" (John 3:31), that is, is exalted above all and, as the beloved Son, preserves His Father's pre-eminence. The Forerunner went on to say, "The Father loveth the Son, and hath given all things into his hand. He that believeth on the Son hath everlasting life: and he that believeth not the Son shall not see life; but the wrath of God abideth on him" (John 3:35–36).

Christ came for baptism partly out of obedience towards the one who sent John. As He said Himself, "Thus it becometh us to fulfil all righteousness" (Matt. 3:15). Other reasons were to make Himself known, to make a beginning of guiding us towards salvation, and to confirm to His followers, who were baptized in accordance with His teaching and commandments, that the Holy Spirit is given in baptism, and that through the Holy Spirit baptism is made a cleansing remedy for the stains sunk deeply into us, because of having been born and living in the passions. Although Christ had no need of cleansing even as man, since He was born of a pure Virgin and lived completely without sin, He was purified for our sake, just as it was for our sake that He had deigned to be born.

Christ was baptized by John, and as He went up from the water the heavens were opened to Him and the voice of the Father was heard from heaven saying, "This is my beloved Son, in whom I am well pleased" (Matt. 3:17). The Spirit of God descended upon Him like a dove, showing those present the one to whom the voice from above bore witness. In this way He was declared to be truly the Son, the Father in heaven was manifested as being truly the Father, and the Spirit too was made known as proceeding from the Father and resting upon the Father's rightful Son. The grace of the Son, of His Father and of the Spirit came to dwell in the baptismal water, such that when it touched those baptized later following His example, they would be divinely regenerated, and mystically renewed and re-created in such a way that they would no longer be from the old Adam and so attract the curse. Instead they would be born of the new Adam and so have God's blessing, not being children of the flesh, but God's children, who were born, not of blood, nor of the will of the flesh, nor of the will of man, but of God through Jesus Christ (John 1:13).

Even if the heavy burden of mortal flesh still weighs them down so as to exercise, test and correct them, and so that they might forsake the wretchedness of this world, invisibly, however, they have put on Christ (Gal. 3:27), so they can strive to share in His manner of life here and now, and afterwards, when they depart hence, to be partakers of His blessedness, radiance and incorruption. Just as through one man, Adam, liability to death passed down by heredity to those born afterwards, so the grace of eternal and heavenly life passed down from the one divine and human Word to all those born again of Him (Rom. 5:12–15, cf. 1 Cor. 15:21–22). Heaven is open to them to receive them in due course if, increasing in faith in God and righteousness according to faith, they receive power to become heirs of God and joint-heirs with Christ, sharing in His incorruptible life and immortality, inseparably united with Him and enjoying His glory (Rom. 8:17–18). Heaven was closed to us before, and we were children of wrath (cf. Eph. 2:3), as God had justly abandoned us because of our sin and disobedience. Through Christ's sinless human nature, however, and His obedience to God (cf. Rom. 5:19), we who hold fast to Christ have become favoured children and beloved sons. Heaven has been opened to us, God's Spirit descends on us and abides in us, and in time we shall be carried up to heaven through Him. He who raised Christ from the dead will quicken our mortal bodies by His Spirit dwelling within us (cf. Rom. 8:11), and transfigure our lowly bodies, making them like Christ's glorious body (cf. Phil. 3:21). Through Christ we have obtained immortality and have been called up to heaven, and our nature is enthroned on the right hand of majesty in heaven far above every principality and power (Eph. 1:21).

O the depth of the riches both of the wisdom and love of God (cf. Rom. 11:33)! In His wisdom, power and love for mankind God knew how to transform incomparably for the better the falls resulting from our self-willed waywardness. If the Son of God had not come down from heaven we should have had no hope of going up to heaven. If He had not become incarnate, suffered in the flesh, risen and ascended for our sake, we should not have known God's surpassing love for us. If He had not taken flesh and endured the passion while we were still ungodly, we should not have desisted from the pride which so often lifts us up and drags us down. Now that we have been exalted without contributing anything, we stay humble, and as we regard with understanding the greatness of God's promise and benevolence we grow in humility; from which comes salvation.

The Son of God became man to show to what heights He would lead us, that we might not be conceited as if we had reversed the defeat by our own efforts. Being twofold in nature, He could truly be a mediator, joining each of the two to the other. He loosed the bond of sin and cleansed the stain that comes of being joined with flesh. He showed God's love for us, and demonstrated that we had sunk so deeply into evil as to make it necessary for God to become flesh. In His flesh and His sufferings He became an example to us of humility and a healing remedy for pride. He made it clear that God created our nature good. He became the author and guarantor of the resurrection and eternal life, delivering us from despair. By becoming the Son of man and sharing our mortality, He made men sons of God and partakers of divine immortality. Human nature was shown to have been created in the image of God, unlike the rest of creation, and this kinship with God was such that human nature could be joined to Him in one person. He honoured this mortal flesh so that the proud spirits should not consider themselves, or be considered, favoured above mankind or as deified because of being without bodies and apparently immortal. He united men and God, who were by nature separate, becoming a mediator through His twofold nature. What more can be said? If the Word of God had not been made flesh, the Father would not have been shown to be truly Father, nor the Son to be truly Son, nor would the Holy Spirit have been shown to shine forth from the Father. God would not have been shown to be essence and hypostases, but would have seemed to be merely some sort of energy observed in creatures, as was said by the foolish sages of old, and now by those who think like Barlaam and Akindynus.

As we have said, the Lord manifested Himself and His plan for our salvation so far as was possible. He revealed the Father as being truly His Father on high. To such as were willing of His contemporaries and those who came after them He indicated the way back to the Father. He urged them on, summoned them and guided them through His way of life, His teaching, His miracles and His prophecies, and even more by His truly divine and supernatural wisdom from which nothing is hidden, either things to come or the obscure movements deep in our hearts. However, those who obeyed Him had to be free of servitude to the devil. Man was led into his captivity when he experienced God's wrath, this wrath being the good God's just abandonment of man. God had to be reconciled with the human race, for otherwise mankind could not be set free from the servitude.

A sacrifice was needed to reconcile the Father on high with us and to sanctify us, since we had been soiled by fellowship with the evil one. There had to be a sacrifice which both cleansed and was clean, and a purified, sinless priest. We needed a resurrection not just of our souls but of our bodies, and a resurrection for those to come after us. This liberation and resurrection, and also the ascension and the everlasting heavenly order, not only had to be bestowed upon us but also confirmed. And all this was necessary not just for those alive at the time and those to come, but also for people born since the beginning of time. In Hades there were far more of such people than there were people to be born later, and far more were to believe and be saved at once. I think that is why Christ came at the end of the ages. He had to preach the gospel to those in Hades (*cf.* 1 Pet. 3:19), to reveal His great plan for salvation to them and to give them complete freedom from the demons who held them captive, as well as sanctification and promises for the future. It was clearly necessary for Christ to descend into Hades, but all these things were done with justice, without which God does not act.

In addition to what we have mentioned, the deceiver had to be justly deceived and to lose the riches he had seized and deceitfully acquired. For evil had taken control through cunning, and the originator of evil continually boasted of this fact. The devil would not have ceased from boasting if he had been subdued by God's sovereign power and not pulled down from his authority by justice and wisdom. Since everybody turns aside to evil in deed or word or thought, or in two or all of these, we defile the purity given by

God to human nature, and need to be sanctified. Sanctification is accomplished by each person's offering and sacrifice of firstfruits, but as the firstfruits have to be pure, we are not able to offer such a sacrifice to God. This is why Christ was revealed, who alone is undefiled and presented Himself as an offering and a sacrifice of firstfruits to the Father for our sake, that all we who look towards Him, believe in Him and attach ourselves to Him through obedience will appear through Him before the face of God, obtain forgiveness and be sanctified. The Lord referred to this in the Gospels, saying, "For their sakes I sanctify myself, that they also might be sanctified through the truth" (John 17:19). Not only did the offering have to be pure and sinless but so did the high priest who offered it. As the apostle says, "Such an high priest became us, who is holy, harmless, undefiled, separate from sinners, and made higher than the heavens" (Heb. 7:26).

For such reasons as these the Word of God was made flesh and dwelt among us, appearing on earth and living with men. He took upon Himself our human flesh, which was subject to suffering and death, even though it was completely pure, and He used it in His divine wisdom as a bait to hook the serpent, the originator of evil, through the Cross, and set free the whole human race which he had enslaved. When a tyrant falls, all those he tyrannized are liberated. This is what the Lord Himself said in the Gospels, that the strong man was bound and his goods spoiled (*cf.* Matt. 12:29). His possessions were taken as spoil by Christ, and were set free, justified, filled with light and endowed with divine gifts. As David sings, "Thou hast ascended on high", up on to the Cross, or, if you wish, up to heaven, "thou hast led captivity captive: thou hast given gifts to men" (Eph. 4:8, *cf.* Ps. 68:18).

Christ overturned the devil through suffering and His flesh which He offered as a sacrifice to God the Father, as a pure and altogether holy victim – how great is His gift! – and reconciled God to our human race. He underwent the passion according to the Father's will and became for us, who were destroyed through disobedience and saved through obedience, an example of how obedient we should be. He showed that death was far more precious than the devil's immortality, because it procured life that was truly immortal, life that will not be subject to the second and eternal death, to the coming damnation, which is worse than ten thousand deaths, but stays with Christ in the heavenly dwellings. When Christ had risen from the dead on the third day and had shown Himself alive to His disciples, He ascended into heaven. He remained immortal and bestowed on us, with complete assurance, resurrection, immortality and truly blessed, eternal, incorruptible life in heaven. By means of the one death and resurrection of His flesh, He healed our twofold death and freed us from our double captivity of soul and body.

When the evil one was justly abandoned by the God of true life because of his voluntary sin, he became a dead spirit. He was the fullness of wickedness, the captain of envy, crafty, and the originator of evil, and he could not bear man to live in the place of delight, that is to say, in paradise. He beguiled him with deadly advice and made him share his own sin and spiritual deadness. Of necessity bodily death followed this spiritual death, so the evil one caused our double death by his single death. Having flung us down even lower than himself, he appeared to be great and exalted, and boasted that he had outwitted us with his intelligence and reduced us to slavery. As he was immortal, he appeared, alas, to be our God. Even after death our souls, having been deserted by God, fell to his lot and he dragged them down into Hades, and shut them up in seemingly inescapable prisons.

God our Creator had mercy upon our wretchedness and graciously willed to descend to the place where we had been thrown, to call us back. He alone appeared free among the dead (Ps. 88:5), descending with His living spirit. Not only that, but He radiated divine light and possessed life-giving power, so that He could enlighten those who sat in darkness and spiritually quicken those in that place who believed in Him. However, on that day when He stands up to raise the whole human race to life and judge it, He will quicken the bodies of all as well. As the leader of the apostles teaches us in his letter, "For this cause was the gospel preached also to them that are dead, that they might be judged according to men in the flesh, but live according to God in the spirit" (1 Pet. 4:6). A little earlier in the epistle he shows us who it was that preached the gospel to the dead in Hades and why, saying, "Christ hath once suffered for sinners, the just for the unjust, that he might bring us to God, being put to death in the flesh, but alive in the spirit: by which also he went and preached unto the spirits in prison" (*cf.* 1 Pet. 3:18–19), that is, to the souls of those who have died since the beginning of time.

As the evil one procured our twofold death by means of his single spiritual death, so the good Lord healed this twofold death of ours through His single bodily death, and through the one resurrection of His body gave us a twofold resurrection. By means of His bodily death He destroyed him who had power over our souls and bodies in death (*cf.* Heb. 2:14), and rescued us from his tyranny over them both. The evil one clothed himself in the serpent to deceive man, but the Word of God put on man's nature to trick the trickster. He received this nature in its undeceived and pure state, and kept it so to the end, offering it as firstfruits to the Father for sanctification from ourselves for ourselves. If the Word of God had not assumed a mortal and passible body, how else could the devil have been deceived, how else would he, who is envy itself, have even dared to attack Him?

The evil one did not attack the Word until he knew that He had a passible body. While He was fasting in the wilderness for forty days He was not hungry – for although He was clothed in a body that could suffer, it only acted and suffered those things proper to a body when permitted to by the almighty power united to it. However, when He had fasted for forty days, according to the Gospel, afterwards He was hungry (Matt. 4:2–11, Luke 4:2–13, *cf.* Mark 1:13). It was exactly then that the originator of evil dared for the first time to attack and set temptation before Him, striving to find a way in to attack His spirit. He was powerfully driven off, and when he made another general assault by means of sensual pleasures, he was mightily defeated and fled away unnerved, shattered and put to shame. Why was he beaten off when, emboldened by the suffering of Christ's body, he attacked? Because he had attempted to introduce sin into the sinless man (*cf.* 1 Tim. 2:5). He fled away shamefully beaten and Christ ceaselessly pursued him, chasing him out of demoniacs, healing diseased people in his power and raising the dead, not just the newly dead, but those already decomposing, and all this by His command alone. He also expelled him from people's souls by preaching repentance and showing that the kingdom of heaven was at hand. He led souls towards faith and a way of life opposed to the enemy, transforming sinners and receiving them. Moreover, He gave His disciples power against demons. Obviously this was completely unendurable for Satan and the angels who fell with him.

If Satan imagined he could drive off the great strength brought to bear against him, would he neglect to do so? Would he tolerate Christ, who cast him out of men and brought down his longstanding tyranny over them, living among men? He rages furiously against Christ, since he knew from experience that His theandric soul was far above all the passions of which he, Satan, was the author, and completely immune from death, which he had created for men by himself. Although Christ's body was both passible and mortal, Satan was not himself able to impose such a death, so he moved the minds of the disobedient Jews towards murdering Him. He provoked them to unrestrained jealousy and fury against Him, because they too had been censured and rejected by Christ as evil. Satan stirred them up and persuaded them to murder Him in a dishonourable way suitable only for criminals and the ungodly, believing that he would thus cast Him out of the world and make His name meaningless on earth. He was confident that when Christ died he would hold His soul imprisoned in hell, just as he had held the souls of all mankind since the beginning of time.

This is how the deceiver was deceived. He attacked Christ's passible and mortal flesh, and unwittingly brought the light into his dark and terrible caverns and set the giver of life over the souls he had tyrannized through spiritual death. Not only that, but he brought those who had died into contact with Christ's body which offered resurrection and immortality, while he was hastening to deliver it to death and the grave. The Lord could have evaded these plots of the devil, but He did not wish to. Rather, it was His will to undergo the passion for our sake, as this was why He became the God-man. Had He not been human, it would not have been possible for Him to suffer; and had He not been God, and remained impassible in His divinity, He could not have suffered death in the flesh for our sake, thereby bestowing upon us resurrection, or rather, rising from the dead and immortality. Nor would it be believable that it was possible for Him not to suffer, but that He chose willingly to do so in order to show that His humility was to liberate us and lift us up, teaching us to wage a practical struggle for righteousness unto death, if need be. To those who believed in the resurrection He proclaimed the power of immortality – not just that they would go on for ever, but that they would continue without eternal destruction, the terrifying eternal damnation prepared for the devil, and live for ever with the holy angels, sharing their enjoyment of the incorruptible and never-ending kingdom.

For this reason the Lord patiently endured for our sake a death He was not obliged to undergo, to redeem us, who were obliged to suffer death, from servitude to the devil and death, by which I mean death both of the soul and of the body, temporary and eternal. Since He gave His Blood, which was sinless and therefore guiltless, as a ransom for us who were liable to punishment because of our sins, He redeemed us from our guilt. He forgave us our sins, tore up the record of them on the Cross and delivered us from the devil's tyranny (*cf.* Col. 2:14–15). The devil was caught by the bait. It was as if he opened his mouth and hastened to pour out for himself our ransom, the Master's Blood, which was not only guiltless but full of divine power. Then instead of being enriched by it he was strongly bound and made an example in the Cross of Christ. So we were rescued from his slavery and transformed into the kingdom of the Son of God. Before we had been vessels of wrath (*cf.* Rom. 9:22–23), but we were made vessels of mercy by Him who bound the one who was strong compared to us, and seized his goods. Then Christ rightly became our King, after being wrongfully murdered at the devil's suggestion, and having mysteriously conquered the originator of evil by righteousness. He clearly demonstrated His almighty power by overcoming bodily death, rising from the dead on the third day, ascending into heaven and sitting on the right hand of the Father together with the flesh which He wore for our sake and in which He died. He proved to us that we would rise from the dead, be restored to heaven and inherit the kingdom if, imitating Him as far as we could, we overthrew the author of sin through righteousness, beating off his attacks and his incitement to evil passions, and courageously bearing his treachery.

The Lord has given us rebirth through divine baptism and sealed us with the grace of the Holy Spirit for the day of redemption (cf. Eph. 4:30), but He has allowed us still to have a body which is mortal and passible. Although He has cast out the teacher of evil from the treasure houses of our soul, yet He allows him to attack from without. This is so that anybody who has been renewed in accordance with the new covenant, that is to say, the gospel of Christ, who lives in good works and repentance, despises the delights of this life, endures suffering and is trained in the enemy's assaults, can be made ready to receive immortality and the incorruptible good things to come in the new age.

Believers should rejoice with hope, and since this life will have an end, should be prudent and glad as they wait with faith for the eternal blessedness of the life to come. They should patiently endure, with the understanding that comes from faith, the wretchedness to which this life has been justly condemned, and resist, by means of long-suffering, sin, its author and ally, and his underlings, to the point of shedding their own blood if need be (cf. Rom. 8:16–18). Except for sin nothing in this life, even death itself, is really evil, even if it causes suffering. The company of the saints brought bodily sufferings upon themselves. The martyrs made the violent death which others inflicted on them into something magnificent, a source of life, glory and the eternal heavenly kingdom, because they exploited it in a good way that pleased God. That is why, when Christ had abolished death by His resurrection, He still let it remain for His followers, along with this life's other misfortunes, so that Christians should be exercised by these means for the sake of truth in both their lives and beliefs, and be made ready through the new covenant for the coming new age which will never grow old.

For those who bear them with faith, these misfortunes serve to correct their sins, to exercise and test them, to lead them to abandon the wretchedness of this life, and to encourage them to long fervently and seek constantly for everlasting adoption as sons and redemption, the truly new life and blessedness. Our adoption as sons and our renewal in Christ in both soul and body is complex. There is a starting point and perfection, and an intermediate stage in between. The grace of baptism, which is called the washing of regeneration, inaugurates this action in us, providing remission of all our sins and of the guilt of the curse. Perfection will come with the resurrection of life for which believers hope, and the promise of the age to come. The intermediate stage is life according to Christ's gospel, by which the godly person is nourished, grows and is renewed, making progress day by day in the knowledge of God, righteousness and sanctification. Gradually he reduces and cuts away his eagerness for things below, and transfers his longing from what is visible, physical and temporary to what is invisible, spiritual and eternal.

The great Paul, eye-witness of unspeakable spiritual mysteries and a chosen vessel, teaches us of this threefold renewal in Christ when he writes in the Epistle to the Romans, "So many of us as were baptized into Christ were baptized into his death. Therefore we are buried with him by baptism into death" (Rom. 6:3–4). This is the beginning of our renewal. Christ tore up the handwriting of our transgressions on the Cross and made all those who were buried with Him through baptism guiltless. Hear also about the intermediate stage after this starting point: "That like as Christ was raised up from the dead by the glory of the Father, even so we also should walk in newness of life" (Rom. 6:4). Then he goes on to refer to the perfection of this renewal, declaring that, "If we have been planted together in the likeness of his death, we shall be also in the likeness of his resurrection" (Rom. 6:5). Later he reveals more clearly both the starting-point and the finish of this renewal and our adoption as sons, saying, "Ourselves, also, which have the firstfruits of the Spirit, even we ourselves groan within ourselves, waiting for the adoption" (Rom. 8:23). By "firstfruits of the Spirit" he means the sanctification and grace of the Spirit, which we receive in holy baptism, when we are delivered from sins, renewed and freely justified by Christ's grace. These are the firstfruits of the good things to come. However, by saying "waiting for the adoption" he shows that he is referring, not to adoption through baptism, but to that future, perfect, unfailing adoption, and he adds, "to wit, the redemption of our body", that is, its redemption from passions and corruption. The adoption of sons which takes place here and now often fails, but that adoption which comes about through bringing the dead back to life and resurrection is truly perfect and sure.

When Paul writes to the Philipians he expresses the aim of this renewal even more clearly, saying, "We look for the Saviour, the Lord Jesus Christ: who shall change our vile body, that it may be fashioned like unto his glorious body" (Phil. 3:20–21). As Christ died in bodily weakness and dishonour, and rose in power and divine glory, so those who live like Christ are sown through death, to quote Paul again, in weakness and dishonour, and are raised in power and glory (*cf.* 1 Cor. 15:43). They receive a glorified, incorruptible body like Christ's after the resurrection when He became the firstborn from the dead (Col. 1:18) and the firstfruits of them that sleep (*cf.* 1 Cor. 15:20). This bodily renewal is seen now through faith and hope rather than with our eyes, not being reality yet. The soul's renewal, on the other hand, begins, as we have said, with holy baptism through the remission of sins and is nourished and grows through righteousness in faith. The soul is continually renewed in the knowledge of God and the virtues associated with this knowledge, and will reach perfection in the future contemplation of God face to face. Now, however, it sees through a glass, darkly (*cf.* 1 Cor. 13:12).

John, whom Christ loved especially, received both types of renewal, of body and of soul, and says, "Now are we the sons of God". This is the starting point of adoption. However, "it doth not yet appear what we shall be: but we know that, when he shall appear, we shall be like him; for we shall see him as he is" (1 John 3:2). This is the perfection of the adoption of sons and renewal which God bestowed on us in Christ, and of which John says in his Gospel that, "Christ gave power to become the sons of God, even to them that believe on his name: which were born, not of blood, nor of the will of the flesh nor of the will of man, but of God" (John 1:12–13).

When he says that we were born not of the flesh but of God, he proclaims regeneration and adoption through holy baptism, and when he says in his epistle, "Now are we sons of God" he means by baptism. On the other hand, when he says that God gave us power to become sons of God, as though we were not yet sons, he is referring to the perfection of adoption. A new born babe has the natural ability to become wise, and is potentially wise, then when he grows older, if he earnestly pursues wisdom, he will actually be wise. In the same way, someone who has been born again through holy baptism has received the ability to be fashioned like the glorious body of the Son of God (*cf.* Phil. 3:21). If he walks in newness of life and lives according to Christ and His gospel, when, in the resurrection, this potential progresses to realization, he will have, not by faith and hope but in truth and reality, a glorified and incorruptible body such as Christ had after the resurrection, and a spirit even more glorious. The dead bodies of the ungodly will also be resurrected, but not in heavenly glory, for they will not be fashioned in the likeness of the glorious body of Christ, nor will they see the vision of God promised to believers, which is called the kingdom of God. "Let the wicked be taken away, that he behold not the glory of the Lord", as the Scripture says (Isa. 26:10 Lxx). But those born and nurtured according to Christ, who, as far as they were able, attained to the measure of the stature of the fullness of Christ (Eph. 4:13), will also obtain the blessing of the divine radiance and will, according to the Scripture, "shine forth as the sun in the kingdom of their father" (Matt. 13:43).

Before the transgression, Adam shared in this divine illumination and brilliance. He was clothed in the true robe of glory and was not naked, nor was he ugly in his nakedness, but was truly unspeakably better adorned than those who wear diadems embellished with much gold and precious stones. When our human nature was stripped of this divine illumination and radiance as a result of the ugly transgression, the Word of God had mercy on this nature and in His compassion took it upon Himself. On Mount Tabor he showed it clothed once more to His chosen disciples (Matt. 17:1–9, Mark 9:2–9, Luke 9:28–37, *cf.* 2 Pet. 1:16–18), proving to all what we had once been, and what those of us who believed in Him and attained to perfection in Him would be through Him in the age to come.

You will find that the earnest of this perfection of those who live according to Christ is openly given here and now to God's saints. They reap already, so to speak, the good of the age to come. Moses foreshadowed this, because the children of Israel could not gaze upon the glory of his face (Exod. 34:30–35). Later, and more clearly, the Lord Himself shone so brightly on the mountain in the divine light that even the chosen disciples, who had received spiritual power from Him, could not stand and look at that radiance (Matt. 17:6, *cf.* Luke 9:34). Stephen's face was like the face of an angel, according to the Scripture (Acts 6:15), and he looked up from earth into the heights of heaven, where Christ sat on the right hand of the majesty, and he saw the heavenly glory of God (Acts 7:55–56). It would take too long to recount and tell at length of the others who received here the earnest of the good things to come and were blessed to obtain this divine illumination and radiance.

May we too attain to this through the grace and love for mankind of our Lord Jesus Christ, who for our sake was made man, suffered, was buried, rose from the dead, took our fallen human nature up to heaven and honoured it by sitting on the Father's right hand. To our Lord Jesus Christ belong glory, honour and worship, together with His Father without beginning and the all-holy and life-giving Spirit, now and for ever and unto the ages of ages. Amen.

On the Sabbath and the Lord's Day

TODAY WE KEEP THE FEAST OF NEW SUNDAY, or rather we celebrate the inauguration of the New Lord's Day. So our word today is intended to reveal a little more of the mystery of Sunday to your charity, as far as time allows. If this is a great and exalted mystery, and not even its more accessible aspects are easy for everyone to understand, we must give thanks to the Lord of all who gave His name to this day, and who, through His coming in the flesh, bestowed on those who draw near to Him through faith things which are perhaps a little difficult for our mind and reason to grasp.

But heed the sense of my words, all of you. And if anyone is unable to understand everything, he will grasp the full meaning from the little he does understand, since the Holy Spirit's teaching is a word of light. In six days God not only made and adorned the whole visible world, He also created and brought to life the only creature with senses and a mind: man (Gen. 1:1–27; 2:7). To him He granted dominion over all the animals and plants throughout the world (Gen. 1:28). Then on the seventh day God rested from all His works, as we are taught by Moses (Gen. 2:2), who was born later, but beheld the foundation of the world long before his time, or rather as the Holy Spirit in His love for mankind sounds in our ears and souls through Moses' words. "And God", it says, "blessed the seventh day and sanctified it" (Gen. 2:3). Why did He bless and hallow that day on which He did nothing? For he did not bless and hallow the first day as the most highly exalted, which is why it was referred to by Moses as "one" and not as "first" (Gen. 1:5 Lxx), that day on which God brought forth everything out of nothing all at once, and illuminated it with new light, although He had not yet put it in due order, assigning everything to its place and kind. And if He did not bless and sanctify that first day, why not the following day, on which He established the great firmament, and stretched out around us the first heaven and after it the second? Then again, why did He not bless the day after that, or the ones following, during which the earth was formed by the waters drawing back and took all nature as its adornment, the heavens received the two great lights for eyes, and the birds and sea creatures took their being from the waters by divine command, each after their kind?

If we leave those days to one side, why did God not bless the sixth day on which He not only drew out of the earth the living souls of reptiles and cattle, but also demonstrated a work worthy of His own Counsel? He crowned the whole of creation, brought together into unity the senses and the mind, greatest of all, put Himself within His creature through His divine grace, and showed man as a living being upon earth in His own image and likeness, capable of knowing Him. So why did He not bless and sanctify that day instead of the seventh, which was a day of inaction? As I want to explain the matter and offer a solution to the problem, I must first, for the sake of the more learned among you gathered here, refute those who have not given a good explanation. There are some, such as Josephus and Philo and their followers, who revere the number seven calling it "unbegotten" (a prime number), and also "virgin" as it does not "beget", or multiply, like, in their opinion, the divinity. For they cannot understand that when God begot the Son He did not set aside virginity, but begot Him without union, variation or passion. Those who contend that these properties of the number seven are the reason why only the seventh day was given God's blessing misrepresent not only God, denying His Fatherhood, but also the number seven itself. Every number originates from units, and since seven is a number it is not "unbegotten". They say, however, that it is not the product of any factors greater than unity, but being unbegotten does not mean not being the product of many, but not being the product of anything at all, which is not the case with the number seven. Furthermore, if the seventh day was blessed because of the properties of that number, it would be much better if the first day had received the blessings, especially as Moses referred to it as "one day". For the number one is completely unbegotten. They object, however, that it produces other numbers and is a factor of every number, including the numbers up to ten, whereas seven is not the factor of any number between one and ten, and is therefore "virgin". Let us say for the sake of argument that to be virgin means not to beget, although this is not necessarily so. If something produces not small but large numbers then clearly the more it produces the further it is from virginity. Now when seven is multiplied or added it does not generate any of the numbers from one to ten, but it does produce many numbers greater than ten. So how can we call it "virgin"? But slipping away from our grasp, these people ascend, as it were, to the moon and the orbits of the stars, of which they say there are seven. They point out that the moon becomes a half moon in seven days and a full moon in a further seven, and wanes in the same manner. For they fail to realize that if the number seven is honourable for such reasons, the other numbers are no less so, especially the first number of all. The whole visible world is one, and so are the heavens, or at most two. There is one sun in the universe and one moon, not to mention that all things were framed by the one God who is before all and through all and above all (cf. Eph. 4:6, Col. 1:16-17, Rom. 9:5), proclaiming the true unity to all who understand aright.

If the stars and their orbits are all spherical and the universe encircles them, this circle has two components: a point and a line, and without these two nothing visible could exist. So two is the number most useful and necessary to the world. However, just as there are not only lines and planes in the universe, so the number three exists, I shall not even mention this number's other advantages. On the other hand, since each of the objects we have mentioned is not just a circle but a solid sphere, they could not exist without the number four, as they have to have another dimension, so four is equally worthy. Similar arguments can be put forward for five, and above all for six. For this is the first of the perfect numbers equal to the sum of its divisors, which is why the world was completed on the sixth day.

Those who hold the number seven in honour for reasons such as these unwittingly honour not just that number but absolutely all of them, since each of them has no lack of similar things which can be said in its favour. Numbers were created by God along with everything else, and everything created by God is good and very good, as the Creator Himself bore witness through Moses (Gen. 1:31). So whatever aspect of numbers you subject to scrutiny you will find good and very good, wonderfully proportioned within itself and in relation to others. But it was not simply their numerical order which distinguished one day from another. In no way did Moses describe God as admiring the products of numbers, but as approving the things He Himself brought forth day by day. Not even the seventh day is praiseworthy because of its number. So now let us tell you why it was that God particularly blessed and hallowed that day, using Moses' words as our starting-point. "And God rested", he says, "on the seventh day from all his work which he had made" (Gen. 2:2). Then he adds that "God blessed the seventh day and sanctified it", and immediately goes on to refer to the reason for this blessing, repeating, "because that in it God had rested from all his works which he had begun to make" (Gen. 2:3 Lxx). So there were certain of God's works which he had neither begun to make nor ceased from making, as the Lord Himself revealed to us, saying, "My Father worketh hitherto, and I work" (John 5:17).

God wanted to impart to us a strong awareness of works of this kind, and to demonstrate that they are more to be sought after than any works perceptible to the senses. So He blessed and sanctified the seventh day, on which He ceased making the visible creation, so that this day might be like an ascent, by means of rest, from things below to those better things above. To quote the great Dionysius,

God, "in His superabundant goodness, goes out of Himself and transcending all things comes down into all things, in accordance with His ecstatic, supraessential power which is inseparable from Him". Condescending in His love for man, as He willed and as was fitting, He made this visible world of ours. Then on the seventh day He went up again, as behoved God, to His own heights, which He had not left, and showed that His rest on that day was still more blessed than what had gone before. In this way He taught us to seek to enter, as far as we are able, into that rest, which is contemplation according to the mind, and ascent to God by that means. The apostle too explicitly urges us towards this rest. Having referred to God's words through the psalmist about the Jewish race, "Unto whom I sware in my wrath that they should not enter into my rest" (Ps. 95:11), he continues, "He spake in a certain place of the seventh day on this wise, And God did rest the seventh day from all his works" (Heb. 4:4). A little further on he writes, "Let us labour therefore to enter into that rest" (Heb. 4:11). For anyone who enters into it, rests from his works as God did from His.

Do you desire to learn more exactly what this rest is, and how we too can enter into it? If we find out which works God did not begin because they were without beginning, we shall better comprehend both this rest and how to enter into it. What are these works? The psalmist and prophet gives us the first part of the answer when he writes of God, "The works of his are verity and judgment" (Ps. 111:7). The knowledge of things that exist and the foreknowledge of things to come are a work of God without beginning, and it would not be wrong to refer to this as verity. Judgment and providence are an unceasing work of God without beginning, for everything that exists required both judgment and providence even before it came into being, since it had to be produced, and once in existence had to be prevented from ceasing to be after a time. It had either, in some cases, eventually to change for its own good or the good of all, or else, in other cases, to remain unchanged. Another of God's works without beginning is the process of returning to Himself, which is motivated by the contemplation of Himself which had no starting point.

If you observe carefully and intelligently, you will find many things which fall into the same category as these divine activities. If, brethren, each of us sets aside our continuous, troublesome, worldly cares and the works associated with them, and sits listening to the Spirit's teaching, firstly he will be praised by the Lord, who did not approve of Martha because she was troubled by many cares, even though her efforts were for His sake. On the other hand, He said that Mary, who sat listening at His feet, had "Chosen the good part, which shall not be taken from her" (Luke 10:41–42).

Do you see what unceasing work means? When you receive into your mind these words of the Spirit's teaching, meditate upon them and prefer them in your soul's reasoning to every other passionate and worldly thought, ordering your life according to them for the sake of your salvation, then you too will have verity and judgment as your work, speaking the truth in your heart, as the psalmist and prophet says (*cf.* Ps. 15:2). If you raise your mind above every thought, however good, and turn it wholly towards itself, by means of constant attention and unceasing prayer, you too will truly enter into the divine rest and obtain the blessing of the seventh day. You will see yourself, and through yourself you will be carried up to the vision of God. For, as it is said, the end of prayer is to be caught up towards the Lord. This is one of the reasons for the blessing of the seventh day, which Moses indicated through the law by commanding that the seventh day be a day of rest – but only of rest from works which benefit the body, for it is a day of activity in the works proper to the soul.

Another reason why that day was blessed is that He who formed this world in six days foresaw that man would turn towards evil and would, as a result, go back to the ground, descend to Hades and be imprisoned there, and this whole world would grow old and useless because of man, but would be renewed by God becoming man. This renewal was effected when God incarnate descended into Hades through death and declared there on the sabbath the recall of souls. It was because He foresaw that this would happen on the sabbath that He rightly deemed it the only day worthy to be blessed. However, although this work was secretly made ready on the seventh day, the sabbath, everything was clearly brought to light and accomplished when the body too had been summoned to immortality through the Lord's resurrection on the eighth day. This is why we call it the Lord's Day. As Friday, the day of preparation, stands in relation to the sabbath, so is the sabbath in comparison with Sunday, which is obviously superior to it. As perfection and reality surpass beginning, pattern and shadow, so is Sunday more excellent and honourable, because on it the exceedingly blessed work was finished, and on it we await the General Resurrection of all, the perfect entry of the saints into the divine rest and dissolution of the world into its elements.

Whatever is said in praise of the seventh day applies even more to the eighth, for the latter fulfils the former. It was Moses who unwittingly first ascribed honour to the eighth day, the Lord's Day. The Jubilee year (Lev. 25:8ff), which Moses regarded as a year of forgiveness and named accordingly, was not counted among the "weeks of years" under the law, but came after them all, and was an eighth year proclaimed after the last of these seven year periods. Moses did the same with regard to periods of seven weeks. However, the lawgiver did not only introduce in this hidden way the dignity of this eighth day, which we call the Lord's Day because it is dedicated to the Lord's resurrection, but also on the feast named "Trumpets" referred to the eighth day as the "final solemn assembly" (*cf.* Lev. 23:36 Lxx, Num. 29:35), meaning the completion and fulfilment of all the feasts. At that point he clearly said that the eighth day too would be called holy for us, proclaiming in advance how divine, glorious and august Sunday was to be after everything pertaining to the law had passed away.

Moses esteemed the seventh day because it led into the truly honourable eighth day. Just as the law given through him is honorable in so far as it leads to Christ (*cf.* Gal. 3:24), so the seventh day is houourable because it leads into the eighth day on which the Lord's resurrection took place. The eighth day comes next after the seventh, and if you look carefully you will find that after the seventh day, when we are told that all the dead from past ages were resurrected, on the eighth day Christ rose. Not only was Christ's resurrection accomplished on the eighth day, but it was both the eighth day in relation to the day before, and also the first day in relation to the hoped-for resurrection, the rising again, of all men in Christ. That is why Christ is hymned as "the firstfruits of them that slept" (1 Cor. 15:20) and "the first begotten of the dead" (Rev. 1:5). In the same way, Sunday is not just the day eighth in order after the preceding days, but the first of the days that come after. So it becomes in its turn the New Day, the first of all days, which we call the Lord's Day, and which Moses referred to not as the first day but as "one day" (Gen. 1:5 Lxx), being exalted above the others and the prelude of the one day without evening of the age to come.

You will understand how much better Sunday is than other feastdays from what follows. Every other festival comes round once a year, but the Lord's Day comes round four times every month, and this frequent recurrence makes the whole year a year of true remission for us, a year acceptable to the Lord (*cf.* Isa. 61:2). It was in order to teach us to celebrate it in practice at the end of each week that the Lord first appeared to the disciples inside the house while Thomas was absent (John 20:19-24). He proved He was alive and gave them peace. By His breathing upon them He renewed the divine breath given in the beginning (Gen. 2:7), and endowed them with the grace of the Holy Spirit, imbuing them with divine power to bind and loose sins. He made them sharers in the exercise of His heavenly lordship, saying to them, "receive ye the Holy Ghost: Whosoever sins ye remit, they are remitted unto them; and whosesoever sins ye retain, they are retained" (John 20:22-23).

The Lord granted them this power and grace when He appeared to them on the very day of His resurrection, obviously a Sunday. Then, letting the intervening days of the week elapse, He appeared in the same manner and in the same house, on the eighth day, the Sunday we celebrate today, to inaugurate His festival and to bring the hesitant Thomas to faith. According to the Saviour's beloved evangelist and disciple, "After eight days again his disciples were within, and Thomas with them: then came Jesus, the doors being shut, and stood in the midst, and said, Peace be unto you" (John 20:26).

You will see that it was Sunday when the disciples assembled and the Lord came to them. On Sunday He approached them for the first time as they were gathered together, and eight days later, when Sunday came round again, He appeared to their assembly. Christ's Church continually reflects these gatherings by holding its meetings mostly on Sundays, and we come among you and preach what pertains to salvation and lead you towards piety and a godly way of life.

Let no one out of laziness or continuous worldly occupations miss these holy Sunday gatherings, which God Himself handed down to us, lest he be justly abandoned by God and suffer like Thomas, who did not come at the right time. If you are detained and do not attend on one occasion, make up for it the next time, bringing yourself to Christ's Church. Otherwise you may remain uncured, suffering from unbelief in your soul because of deeds or words, and failing to approach Christ's surgery to receive, like the divine Thomas, holy healing. There exist not only thoughts and words of faith but also deeds and acts of faith – "Shew me", it says, "thy faith by thy works" (cf. Jas. 2:18) – and if someone abandons these and is completely distanced from the Church of Christ and given over wholly to worthless pursuits, his faith is dead, or non-existent, and he himself has become dead through sin.

But are some of you puzzled that Christ could enter when the doors were shut, since He had a body? Apparently you are unaware that spiritual things must be compared with spiritual and understood on their own terms, as the holy apostle says (cf. 1 Cor. 2:13). Christ did not spoil the womb of the Virgin who bore Him in the flesh. He did not undo the signs of virginity when He was born, but kept them intact, even though at that time His body was subject to suffering and death. So it is not at all surprising if now that He had immortalized the humanity He had assumed and His body was no longer subject to death, He could enter through closed doors. However, as He undoubtedly had a body free from suffering and death, how was it that on His Side and His Hands He had marks of wounds and holes from the nails? For the evangelist tells us that the Lord said to Thomas, "Reach hither thy finger, and behold my hands; and reach hither thy hand, and thrust it into my side: and be not faithless, but believing" (John 20:27). Why did He have scars? It would be impossible for a mortal, suffering body to display marks of wounds and nails and to remain healthy and sound. On the other hand, an immortal body without suffering can show the scars and wounds it suffered to anyone at will, and nevertheless continue free from suffering and death.

This enables me to understand something else: that those who have suffered for Christ are adorned for ever with their wounds. Windows in a house do not make it less safe and are not something ugly but a necessary decoration for a building, to let in light and allow those within to look out. In the same way, the body's sufferings for Christ's sake and the resultant wounds become for those who bear them windows to let in the light without evening. And when that light shines forth they will be recognizable by the divine beauty and radiance of their wounds and not by their ugliness. Their scars will not be obliterated when suffering comes to an end, in so far as they procure immortality.

Christ's body held within it the fount of divine light, which shone forth spiritually to enlighten the mind of him who hesitated, so that Thomas cried out at once, with perfect theology, "My Lord and my God" (John 20:28). The Lord said to him, "Because thou hast seen me, thou hast believed: blessed are they that have not seen, and yet have believed" (John 20:29), showing that those who saw the Lord with their own eyes are not in greater glory than those who have been brought through them to faith in Him. He did not say "yet believe" but "yet have believed", because with the divine power of foreknowledge whereby He saw everything before it happened, future events were like present facts.

I shall tell you, in your charity, something which has just occurred to me. I notice that Thomas lost his faith when he was absent, but when he was together with the believers his faith did not in any way fall short. So I have the idea that if only a sinner will flee the company of immoral men and associate with the just, he will never be found lacking in righteousness or the resultant salvation of his soul. It seems to me that the psalmist and prophet was hinting at this when he called blessed the man who avoided sitting with the scornful and being their companion (*cf.* Ps. 1:1). Another prophet writes, "Thou shalt not follow the multitude to do evil" (Exod. 23:2), and the author of Proverbs says, "Where sinners gather, the fire breaks out" (Ecclus. 16:6), "but he that walketh with wise men shall be wise" (Prov. 13:20).

So let us, brethren, meet together and often come to God's Church, where all who are truly godly are present and never stay away. When each of you enters the church, look for the more godly of those within, whom you can recognize just by seeing how they stand in attentive silence. Watch for those who are more pious and God-fearing than the rest, and go and attach yourself to them, and attend upon God with them. When you come out after the dismissal on the Lord's Day and are at leisure from earthly work for the sake of Him whose day it is, carefully search to see if there is an imitator of the apostles who mostly stays indoors, longing for God with silent prayer, psalmody and other suitable practices. Approach such a person and enter his small room with faith as though you were entering a heavenly place containing the Spirit's sanctifying power. Sit down beside him and stay with him as long as possible. Talk to him about God and divine matters, asking questions, humbly learning and appealing for help through prayer. If you do this, I know for sure that Christ will invisibly come to you, give peace within the thinking part of your soul, increase your faith, strengthen your steadfastness, and in due time set you among His chosen in the heavenly kingdom.

May we all attain to this in Him who has now died and risen for us and afterwards will come in glory, Christ the King of the ages, to whom belongs glory unto the ages of ages. Amen.

On the Ascension of Christ I

THE JEWS KEPT THE FEAST of the Passover, the crossing from Egypt to the land of Palestine, as laid down in their law, and we have celebrated the gospel Pascha, the passage of our human nature in Christ from death to life (*cf.* John 5.24, 1 John 3:14), from corruption to incorruption (*cf.* 1 Cor. 15:42, 50). What words can express the superiority of this celebration over the solemnities of the old law and the events commemorated on its holy days? No one can adequately state how much more excellent it is. The enhypostatic Wisdom of the most high Father, God's pre-eternal Word who is beyond all being, who was united with us in His love for mankind and lived among us (*cf.* John 1:14), has now revealed through His actions a cause for celebration even more distinctly superior than Easter's excellence. For we now celebrate the transition of our nature in Him, not just from the subterranean regions up on to the earth, but from the earth to the heaven of heavens, and to the throne above the heavens of Him who rules over all.

Today the Lord not only stood with His disciples after His resurrection, but was also parted from them and was taken up into heaven as they watched (Acts 1:9–11), ascended and entered into the true Holy of Holies and sat down on the right hand of the Father, far above all principality and power and every name and honour that is known and named, either in this world, or in that which is to come (*cf.* Eph. 1:20–21). There were many resurrections before Christ's resurrection, and similarly, there were many ascensions before His ascension. The Spirit lifted up Jeremiah the prophet, and an angel took up Habakkuk (Bel & Dr. 33–39 Lxx). In particular it is written that Elijah went up with a chariot of fire (2 Kgs. 2:11). But even he did not go beyond the realms of earth, and the ascension of each of those mentioned was just a sort of movement lifting them up from the ground without taking them out of the area surrounding the earth. Similarly, the others who were resurrected all died and returned to the earth. By contrast, Christ has risen and death no longer has dominion over Him (*cf.* Rom. 6:9), and now He has ascended and sat down on high, every height is below Him and bears witness that He is God over all (Rom. 9:5).

The Master's body is the visible mountain of which Isaiah speaks, the Lord's house above the tops of all the mountains of reason (*cf.* Isa. 2:2 Lxx). Neither an angel nor a man, but the incarnate Lord Himself came and saved us, being made like us for our sake while remaining unchanged as God. In the same way as He came down, without changing place but condescending to us, so He returns once more, without moving as God, but enthroning on high our human nature which He had assumed. It was truly right that the first begotten human nature from the dead (Rev. 1:5) should be presented there to God, as firstfruits from the first crop offered for the whole race of men.

Although many resurrections and ascensions have taken place, we celebrate none of them as we do the Lord's resurrection and ascension, because we neither have nor ever shall have any share in those others. All we gained from them was to be led towards faith in our Saviour's resurrection and ascension, in which we all share now and in the future. His resurrection and ascension are the resurrection and ascension of our human nature; and not just of our human nature, but of everyone who believes in Christ and shows his faith in works (*cf.* Jas. 2:18). Christ was unbegotten and uncreated according to His divinity, and it was for our sake that He became man. He lived as He did because of us, teaching us the path that leads back to true life. Everything He suffered in the flesh He suffered for us to heal our passions. On account of our sins He was led to death, and for us He rose and ascended, preparing our own resurrection and ascension for unending eternity. For all the heirs of everlasting life follow as far as possible the pattern of His saving work on earth.

We start this imitation of Christ with holy baptism, which symbolizes the Lord's burial and resurrection. Virtuous living and conduct in accord with the gospel are its intermediate stage, and its perfection is victory through spiritual struggles against the passions, which procures painless, indestructible, heavenly life. As the apostle tells us: "If ye live in the flesh, ye shall die: but if ye through the Spirit do mortify the deeds of the body, ye shall live" (*cf.* Rom. 8:13). Those who live according to Christ imitate what He did in the flesh. Just as He died physically, so in time everyone dies, but we shall also rise again in the flesh as He did, glorified and immortal, not now but in due course, when we shall also ascend, as Paul says: for "we shall be caught up", he says, "in the clouds, to meet the Lord in the air: and so shall we ever be with the Lord" (1 Thess. 4:17).

Do you see that any of us who wishes will share in the Lord's resurrection, and will be an heir of God and joint-heir with Christ (*cf.* Rom. 8:17)? That is why we joyfully celebrate the resurrection of our human nature, its exaltation and sitting down on high, and also the starting point of the resurrection and ascension of each of the faithful, publicly proclaiming the words of today's Gospel reading, that when the Lord had risen, He stood in the midst of His disciples (Luke 24:36–53).

Why did He stand in their midst and afterwards accompany them? "And he led them out", it says, "as far as to Bethany, and he lifted up his hands, and blessed them" (Luke 24:50). He did it to show that He was completely whole and unharmed, to prove that His feet, that had endured being pierced by nails, were sound and trod firmly, that His hands, that had been likewise nailed to the Cross, and His side, that had been pierced by the spear, were whole, even though they bore the signs of the wounds as confirmation of the saving passion. I think that the words, "He stood in the midst of his disciples" (*cf.* Luke 24:36), also imply that their faith in

Him was strengthened by the way He appeared and blessed them. He did not just stand among them all, but stood in the midst of each one's heart and it was strengthened through faith, so that the psalmist's words, "God is in the midst of her; she shall not be moved" (Ps. 46:5), can be applied to each of their hearts. For from then on the Lord's apostles became steadfast and immovable.

So He stood in the midst of them and said: "Peace be unto you" (Luke 24:36), that sweet, penetrating and familiar salutation. There are two kinds of peace: peace with God, which is above all the fruits of godliness, and peace with one another, which arises naturally from the words of the Gospel. At that time the Lord gave them both by His one greeting. When He first sent them out He told them, "Into whatsoever house ye enter, first say, Peace be to this house" (Luke 10:5). Now He did exactly that, and entering the house where they were gathered, He straightway gave them peace. He saw that they were frightened and troubled by the unexpected and strange sight – "and supposed", it says, "that they had seen a spirit" (Luke 24:37), that is, that the person they saw was a phantom. So once more He told them what was happening in their own hearts, revealed that He was the one to whom they had said before the passion and resurrection, "Now are we sure that thou knowest all things, and needest not that any man should ask thee" (John 16:30), and proposed that they reassure themselves by examining and touching Him. Once He saw that they had accepted the truth, He gave further confirmation for them to scrutinize by taking food while they watched, as well as sharing fellowship and peace with them. "And while they yet believed not and wondered", certainly not because they dissented, but for joy, "he said unto them, Have ye here any meat? And they gave him a piece of a broiled fish, and of an honeycomb. And he took it, and did eat it before them" (Luke 24:41–43).

That incorruptible body was fed after the resurrection, not because it needed food, but to prove it had risen and to demonstrate that it was the same one as had eaten with them before the passion. It did not, however, consume the food in the way that mortal bodies do, but by divine energy, as, so to speak, fire dissolves wax, except that fire has to have fuel to sustain it, whereas immortal bodies do not need food for sustenance.

The piece of baked fish and the honeycomb which He ate were also symbols of Christ's mystery. The Word of God united Himself hypostatically with our human nature, which was like a fish swimming in the water of pleasure-loving, passionate life. By the unapproachable divine fire of His Godhead He cleansed this nature of every tendency towards passion, and made it equal to God, and, as it were, red hot. The Lord came to send fire upon the earth (*cf.* Luke 12:49), and through participation in this fire He makes divine not just the human substance which He assumed for our sake, but every person who is found worthy of communion with Him. On the other hand, human nature is like honeycomb because we hold the treasure of reason in our bodies, just as honey is contained in the comb. This is especially true of anyone who believes in Christ, for he has the grace of the divine Spirit stored up in his soul and body like honey in wax. The Lord ate these things because he was pleased to take the salvation of each human being as His food. He did not, however, eat it all, but just a piece of a honeycomb, that is, a part of it, for not everyone believed. Nor did He take this portion Himself, but it was given Him by His disciples, for the disciples set before Him just the believers, separating them from the faithless.

By eating the fish and the honeycomb in front of His disciples in this way and for these reasons, He reminded them of the words He spoke to them previously when He was approaching His passion, thus proving that He was truthful. What He had foretold was fulfilled, and He opened their understanding, that they might understand the Scriptures and know that thus it behoved God's only-begotten Son to be made man for men's sake on account of the unfathomable ocean of His love, to be manifested and witnessed to by the Father's voice from above and the appearance of the divine Spirit (*cf.* Luke 3:22). It was fitting that He be proved worthy of trust and admiration by extraordinary acts and words, and also that He be envied and betrayed by people who did not seek God's glory but honour from men, that He should be crucified, buried and rise on the third day from the dead. Repentance and the remission of sins had to be preached in His name, beginning at Jerusalem (Luke 24:47). Those who saw Him with their own eyes and served Him were to become messengers and witnesses of these events. He proclaimed that He would send them from above the promise of His Father, the Holy Spirit, and He ordered them to stay in Jerusalem until they were endued with power from on high (Luke 24:49).

As He spoke in this way to His disciples of matters pertaining to salvation, He led them out of the house and as far as Bethany, and when He had blessed them, He was parted from them and carried up to heaven (Luke 24:50–51). With a radiant cloud for a chariot, He ascended in glory (*cf.* Acts 1:9), entered the Holy of Holies not made by hands and sat down on the right hand of the heavenly majesty, making our human substance share His own throne and divinity. As the apostles continued looking steadfastly towards heaven, they learnt authoritatively from angels that He would come again from heaven in the same way with everyone watching (Acts 1:10). The Lord Himself foretold this, and earlier Daniel had seen it. "I saw", he said, "and behold, one like the Son of man came with the clouds of heaven" (Dan. 7:13). The Lord Himself said, "All the tribes of the earth shall see the Son of man coming in the clouds of heaven" (*cf.* Matt. 24:30).

The disciples worshipped the most high Lord who had come down from above the heavens, made the earth into heaven and gone up again whence He came, having united things below with things above and formed one Church, at the same time heavenly and earthly, to the glory of His love for mankind. Then they returned with joy from the Mount of Olives, whence the Master had ascended, to Jerusalem and were continuously in the Temple with their minds set on heaven, praising and blessing God (Luke 24:53), and preparing themselves to receive the promised coming of the divine Spirit.

Briefly put, brethren, that is how those called by Christ's name should order their lives. They should persevere in prayers and supplications and, in imitation of the angels, have their eyes lifted up to the Master above the heavens, praising and blessing

Him with irreproachable conduct, and waiting for His mystical coming. As the psalmist says to Him, "I will sing and will behave myself wisely in a perfect way. O when wilt thou come unto me?" (Ps. 101:2). Paul demonstrated this too by saying, "For our conversation is in heaven" (Phil. 3:20), "whither the forerunner is for us entered, even Jesus" (Heb. 6:20). Peter, the chief apostle, also guides us in this direction: "Gird up the loins of your mind", he says, "be perfectly sober, and hope for the grace that is to be brought unto you at the revelation of Jesus Christ" (1 Pet. 13:8), "whom having not seen, ye love" (1 Pet. 1:8). The Lord too hinted at the same with His words, "Let your loins be girded about, and your lights burning; and ye yourselves like unto men that wait for their Lord, when he will return" (Luke 12:35–36). In this way He did not destroy the sabbath but fulfilled it, showing that the day of rest from physical work for the sake of what is more excellent, is a truly blessed sabbath. It is linked with a blessing because when we are at leisure from earthly labours which are soon to cease, we wait patiently on God, seeking what is heavenly and imperishable with unashamed hope.

Under the old law one day of the week was the sabbath, and the Lord seemed to the foolish Jews to destroy what they thought of as their day of rest. However, He said, "I am not come to destroy the law, but to fulfil" (Matt. 5:17). How was it that He did not do away with this sabbath but fulfilled the law regarding it? He promised to give the Holy Spirit to those who asked Him (*cf.* Luke 11:13) by day and by night, and commanded them to be always awake and watching, saying, "Be ye ready: for in such an hour as ye think not the Son of man cometh" (Matt. 24:44). In this way He made all the days into blessed sabbaths for those who choose to obey Him perfectly, and so in this respect as well He did not abolish but fulfilled the law.

We, by contrast, are entangled in worldly affairs, but if you abstain from acquisitiveness and mutual hatred, and strive to speak the truth and be chaste, then you too will make every day a sabbath by being inactive in evil. When a day comes that is especially profitable for salvation, you must free yourselves even from blameless work and words, patiently stay in God's Church, listen with understanding to the reading and teaching and contritely attend to the supplications, prayers and hymns to God. Thus you too will fulfil the sabbath, ordering your conduct according to the gospel of God's grace and lifting up the eyes of your understanding towards Christ sitting above the vaults of heaven with the Father and the Spirit. He has made us sons of God, not sons adopted in name alone (*cf.* Rom. 8:14–17), but having become members of one family with God and each other in the communion of the divine Spirit, through Christ's own body and blood.

Let us preserve this union with one another by indissoluble love. We should always look towards our Father in heaven, for we are no longer "of the earth, earthy", like "the first man", but like "the second man, the Lord from heaven" (1 Cor. 15:47). "As is the earthy, such are they also that are earthy: and as is the heavenly such are they also that are heavenly. And as we have borne the image of the earthy, we shall also bear the image of the heavenly" (1 Cor. 15:48–49). As we lift up our hearts to Him we shall behold the great spectacle of our nature united for ever with the fire of the divinity. And laying aside everything to do with the coats of skins in which we were clothed because of the transgression (*cf.* Gen. 3:21), let us stand on holy ground (*cf.* Exod. 3:5), each one of us marking out his own holy ground through virtue and steadfast inclination towards God.

In this way we shall be bold when God comes in fire, and run forward to be enlightened and once enlightened live with Him for ever, to the glory of Him who is the light above all, the threefold Sun and sovereign brightness, to whom belong all glory, might, honour and worship, now and for ever and unto the ages of ages. Amen.

On the Ascension of Christ II

DO YOU SEE THIS SHARED CELEBRATION and joy of ours, which the Lord bestowed on those who believe in Him with His resurrection and ascension? It sprang from affliction. Do you see this life, or rather, this immortality? It shone upon us through death. Do you see the heavenly height to which Christ ascended when He was taken up, and the sublime glory with which He was glorified according to the flesh? He attained to this by means of humility and dishonour. As the apostle says of Him, "He humbled himself and became obedient unto death, even the death of the cross. Wherefore God hath highly exalted him, and given him a name which is above every name: that at the name of Jesus every knee should bow, of things in heaven, and things in earth, and things under the earth; and that every tongue should confess that Jesus Christ is Lord, to the glory of God the Father" (Phil. 2:8–11).

If, then, God highly exalted His Christ because He humbled Himself, suffered dishonour, was tempted and endured a shameful Cross and death for our sake, how will He save, glorify and raise us up if we neither choose humility, nor show love to our fellows, nor gain our souls by enduring temptation (*cf.* Luke 21:19), nor follow the saving Guide through the "strait gate" and along the "narrow way" leading to eternal life (Matt. 7:14)? To this we were called, says

Peter, the chief apostle, "Because Christ also suffered for us, leaving us an example that we should follow his steps" (cf. 1 Pet. 2:21). But why is it that God's Christ went through such sufferings? Why did God highly exalt Him on that account, and why does He call us to share in His Son's sufferings? God alone is always the same, before all ages and unto all ages, and remaining ever unchanged. He has no beginning and no end. He neither comes into being nor suffers corruption, neither increases nor decreases. He does not alter in any way or move from place to place. He has no origin and is uncreated, immutable, unconfused and uncircumscribed. He turns all things to the best as He wills, and permits whatever suffers change for the worse to do so. Anything with a beginning is necessarily subject to change, since a beginning is a sort of change. All creation, therefore, is liable to change: creatures visible and invisible, with or without senses or reason. Only reasonable natures have free will, and can turn to the good or the bad voluntarily by themselves. They either attach themselves to God's will, which results in their continuous progress, improvement and advancement, or they oppose God's will, are justly subjected to what He permits, and sink wretchedly from bad to worse.

Two types of reasonable beings were created by God: firstly the immaterial angels, then material human beings. Neither of these, however, remained in obedience to their Creator and natural Master. The heavenly ranks of immaterial angels, which were created first, were the first to suffer from the disease of apostasy from God. Those angels who stood aloof from this disease are light, and are always being filled full of light, becoming ever more radiant and making blessed use of their natural ability to change. They dance for joy around the first light, look continuously towards Him and are enlightened directly by Him, as they tirelessly sing the praises of the fount of light and, being ministers of light, transmit illuminating grace to those lower beings who are being enlightened.

When Satan, who broke away and refused to obey God, fell from the light, embraced darkness and was condemned to eternal gloom, he became a vessel of darkness, its creator, author and minister, initially for himself and the angels who fell with him, then, alas, also for us in God's paradise, when we rebelled against God and believed the devil. However, all the wicked angels are darkness in themselves and did not become evil just by sharing the devil's darkness. They are the origin and perfection of disobedience, the bitter root and source of all sin, and in particular, they were the cause of our own transgression. Therefore their sin is unpardonable, they grow ever more uncontrollably dark, progress towards their own destruction and will not return to the Enlightener of angels and men. As we, by contrast, did not become evil on our own initiative, God's chastening came upon us with mercy from the beginning. Although we have been condemned to death, it comes after that period of many years appointed for repentance, which Adam survived after the transgression and which each one of us must undergo.

From this it can be clearly seen that we are not without hope of salvation, nor is it at all the right time for us to despair. All our life is a season of repentance, for God "desires not the death of the sinner", as it is written, "but that the wicked turn from his way and live" (*cf.* Ezek. 33:11 Lxx). For, if there were no hope of turning back, why would death not have followed immediately on disobedience, and why would we not be deprived of life as soon as we sin? For where there is hope of turning back, there is no room for despair.

It is attested that Adam's son Abel seemed well-pleasing and acceptable to God in the very beginning (*cf.* Gen. 4:4). Then not long after our fall, Enos "hoped to call upon the Lord" (*cf.* Gen. 4:26 Lxx). As for Enoch, he not only pleased God but was also taken by Him (Gen. 5:24), becoming a clear sign of His compassions towards us fallen men. Once more sin gained momentum, and once more God turned away from the human race and we were justly given over to a universal flood. But yet again His wrath was not unmitigated, nor His judgment merciless. God found Noah righteous in his generation (Gen. 6:9ff), and miraculously preserved him as a second root of mankind, as if He were providentially pruning the human race as it ran wild, but not destroying it by cutting it down or uprooting it. Afterwards Abraham was clearly faithful and well-pleasing to

God, as He Himself bore witness (*cf.* Gen. 22:16–18). Later came his son Isaac, Isaac's son Jacob, and Jacob's sons the patriarchs, who received promises and prophecies of more excellent mercy and divine love that would powerfully overcome our sins, in that the great Shepherd Himself would come down from holy heaven to seek the lost sheep. Subsequently there appeared lawgivers, judges, and a royal line from which it was promised that Christ would come openly in the flesh.

Now Christ has come and been manifested, the pre-eternal Word of God who created us in the beginning. He became like us for our sake in order to renew and re-create those who had grown old and been crushed by sin. Since our ruin was voluntary and our own doing, in His wisdom and love He brought about our renewal in that humanity which He assumed for our sake from the Virgin's womb. He fulfilled the whole mysterious plan of salvation, enabled us to return through His own union with us, opened up a road to heaven for us through the way He lived, and showed us this upward path by His teaching.

Since illnesses are cured by their opposite remedies, as we had been put to death by the wicked counsel of the evil one, we were made alive again by the good counsel of the good Lord. The deadly counsellor had at his disposal pleasure, glory and comfort, which enchanted mankind and dragged it down. So the Counsellor of true life Himself led the way along the strait and narrow way which leads to life above, and guided us in it. "Strive", He says, "to enter in at the strait gate" (Luke 13:24), and "strait and narrow is the way which leadeth unto life, for wide and broad is the way that leadeth to destruction" (*cf.* Matt. 7:13–14). Elsewhere He warns more clearly against that path, saying, "Woe unto you that are rich! Woe unto you, that are full! Woe unto you, when all men shall speak well of you" (*cf.* Luke 6:24–26), thus declaring wretched all lovers of glory, pleasure and money. Again He says, "Lay not up for yourselves treasures upon earth" (Matt. 6:19), and "Take heed to yourselves, lest at anytime your hearts be overcharged with surfeiting, and drunkenness, and cares of this life" (Luke 21:34), and "How can ye believe, which receive honour one of another, and seek not the honour that cometh from God only?" (John 5:44).

With such words as these He snatches us back from the way leading to death, whereas in other places He demonstrates how blessed the way is that leads to life: "Blessed are the poor. Blessed are the merciful. Blessed are they which are persecuted for righteousness' sake" (*cf.* Matt. 5:3–10), and "Sell that thou hast, and give to the poor, and thou shalt have treasure in heaven" (Matt. 19:21), and, "Everyone that hath left house, or lands, or any other earthly goods, for my sake, and the gospel's, shall receive an hundredfold and inherit eternal life" (*cf.* Mark 10:29–30, Matt. 19:29). He clamped down on anger to the extent that He declared it equal to murder and subject to the same condemnation, and said that anyone moved by anger to insult someone was in danger of hell-fire (*cf.* Matt. 5:22). On the other hand, He not only pronounced meekness blessed, but honoured it with the greatest rewards (Matt. 5:5). He condemned licentiousness so severely that He called a passionate, inquisitive glance at another man's wife adultery (*cf.* Matt. 5:28), whereas He emphasized that anyone who acted with purity would be blessed, and afterwards see God (Matt. 5:8). Did He not show how unacceptable perjury was by forbidding even oaths that were faithfully kept, and regarding everything except "yes" and "no" as from the evil one? "Let your communication", He said, "be, Yea, yea; Nay, nay: for whatsoever is more than these cometh of evil" (Matt. 5:37). Why did He repeat the words "yea" and "nay"? The "yes" or "no" we utter has to be in agreement with the facts. Then "yes" will be "yes" and "no", "no". Otherwise, "yes" will be "no" and "no" will be "yes", which obviously comes from the devil. For "when he speaketh a lie, he speaketh of his own: for he is a liar" and "does not abide in the truth" (John 8:44).

In this way the Lord restricted and curbed our words and actions, and enclosed our lives in truth, righteousness, purity and freedom from anger. How does He advise us, though, to behave towards those who are angry with us and oppose us in word and deed and oppress us? "Overcome", says the Scripture, "evil with good" and "give place unto wrath" (Rom. 12:21, 19). "Resist not evil" (Matt. 5:39) and "recompense to no man evil for evil" (Rom. 12:17), or insult for insult, but "Love your enemies, bless them that curse you, do good to them that hate you, and pray for them which despitefully use you, and persecute you" (Matt. 5:44). What will be the outcome of this life of constraint and the reward for these struggles? "That ye may be", it says, "children of your Father which is in heaven" (Matt. 5:45), "heirs of God and joint-heirs with Christ" (Rom. 8:17); that you may have immortal life and receive an ineffable, unshakable, unending kingdom, living and reigning with God for endless ages.

Do you see what the strait and narrow way is, why we are asked to follow it, and to what glory, joy and reward it leads anyone choosing to go along it? If someone promised to give you long life if only you obeyed him, would you not eagerly submit to him, provided he did not demand anything impossible? If, moreover, he promised health, glory and pleasure for as long as you lived, is there anything you would not undertake for him? And if he offered a kingdom that was free from wars and untroubled as well as a long, healthy life, would you not be thrilled and think easy everything grievous that led to that end, sustaining yourself with expectations and enjoying the object of your hope as if it were already present, as long as you considered he was telling the truth?

Given that we desire long life, should we not take eternal life into account? If we long for a kingdom which, however enduring, has an end, and glory and joy which, great as they are, will fade, and wealth that will perish with this present life, and we labour for the sake of such things; ought we not to seek the kingdom, glory, joy and riches which, as well as being all-surpassing, are unfading and endless, and ought we not to endure a little constraint in order to inherit it? Besides, we are presupposing a kingdom free from war, which is impossible on earth, and a life without sorrow, which you can only find in heaven. So let anyone who desires these things run towards heaven and, whether the way there be easy or difficult, let him journey along it, "rejoicing in hope" and "patient in tribulation" (Rom. 12:12).

You all know for what sort of reasons people subject themselves to hardship and death. Is a soldier not prepared to risk deadly danger and slaughter for his modest pay? For a small profit does the merchant not despise shipwreck, gales and violent men that cause damage at sea and on land? Does it not often happen that people become slaves of inhuman masters for the sake of a little bread? So shall we not serve the Lord who by nature loves mankind, risk our lives and get rid of superfluous possessions in order to acquire heavenly riches? Shall we not endure dishonour from men, usually scoundrels, so as to attain to divine glory, exchanging the mortal for the immortal? Shall we not be hungry in moderation and thirsty, that we may eat the bread of life which came down from heaven (John 6:51) and drink the true living water, whosoever is worthy to eat and drink of which, shall never hunger or thirst (John 4:10, 14)? Should we not cleanse the eye of our soul, abstaining "from all defilement of the flesh and spirit" (2 Cor. 7:1), in order that we may see that light which preceded the sun, or rather, that we become children of that light (Eph. 5:8), and other lights ourselves, through sharing in His light, holding forth the word of life (*cf.* Phil. 2:15–16)?

Brethren, I entreat you, let us not prefer darkness to light, the devil to God, that pleasure which is the servant of death and hell to eternal divine joy. Let us not choose destruction's abundant possessions, which, as the Lord showed us through the parable of the Rich Man (Luke 16:19ff), are fuel for the flame which eternally burns those who acquired wealth in an evil way, rather than the love that enriches. Instead, let us live as He did, and as He showed and taught us when He was made man. Let us take up our cross and follow Him (Matt. 16:24), having crucified the flesh with its passions and desires (Gal. 5:24), that we may be glorified together with Him (Rom. 8:17), and rise with Him, and after our resurrection be taken up to Him, as He was taken up today to the Father. He was standing in the midst of the disciples, as Luke says (Luke 24:36), or rather, He appeared to them, as Mark records (Mark 16:14) – for He did not arrive at the moment He appeared, but was always with them and showed Himself visibly when He wished. So, as He was standing in the midst of His disciples He ordered them to preach (Mark 16:15), gave them the promise of the Holy Spirit (Luke 24:49) and declared that He would be with them to the end (Matt. 28:20). After these words, He lifted up His hands and blessed them, and was taken up as they watched (Luke 24:50–51). In this way He showed that those who obeyed Him would also be carried up to God after rising again.

He was separated from them in the body (though as God He was with them) and, as He had promised them, He was taken up and sat on the right hand of the Father with our human flesh. As He lived, died, rose and ascended, so we all live, die and are resurrected. Not all of us, however, will attain to the ascension, but only those for whom to live is Christ, and to die for Him is gain (Phil. 1:21), those who, before they died, crucified sin through repentance and a way of life in accord with the gospel. After the resurrection of all, they alone will be caught up in the clouds to meet the Lord in the air (*cf.* 1 Thess. 4:17). A cloud also received the Lord as He ascended, as Luke relates in the Acts of the Apostles (Acts 1:9). After the ascension the disciples did not see Him with their bodily eyes but with the eyes of their souls, yet they worshipped Him (Luke 24:52). Let us do the same, then, like them, stay in peace (for Jerusalem means peace) keeping peace within ourselves and with one another. Let each of us go into our own upper room (Acts 1:13), our mind, and stay there praying, and let us purify ourselves from passionate and base thoughts.

In this way we shall not miss the coming of the Comforter, and shall worship the Father, Son and Holy Spirit in spirit and in truth, now and for ever and unto the ages of ages. Amen.

On Pentecost

A SHORT WHILE AGO, with the strong eyes of faith, we beheld Christ ascending, no less clearly than those accounted worthy to be eye-witnesses, nor are we less favoured than they. "Blessed are they that have not seen, and yet have believed", says the Lord (John 20:29), referring to those who have found assurance through hearing, and see by faith. Recently we saw Christ lifted up from the ground bodily (Acts 1:9). Now, through the Holy Spirit sent by Him to His disciples, we see how far Christ ascended and to what dignity He carried up the nature He assumed from us. Clearly He went up as high as the place from which the Spirit sent by Him descended. He who spoke through the prophet Joel showed us whence the Spirit comes, saying, "I will pour out my spirit upon all flesh" (Joel 2:28), and to Him David addressed the words, "Thou sendest forth thy spirit, they are created: and thou renewest the face of the earth" (Ps. 104:30). It follows that at His ascension Christ went up to the Father on high, as far as His Fatherly bosom, from which comes the Spirit. Having been shown, even in His human form, to share the Father's glory, Christ now sent forth the Spirit who comes from the Father and is sent by Him from heaven. But when we hear that the Spirit was sent by the Father and the Son, this does not mean that the

Spirit has no part in their greatness, for He is not just sent, but also Himself sends and consents to be sent. This is clearly shown by Christ's words spoken through the prophet, "Mine hand hath laid the foundation of the earth and stretched out the heavens, and now the Lord God, and His Spirit, hath sent me" (cf. Isa. 48:13–16). Again, speaking through the same prophet He says, "The Spirit of the Lord is upon me; because the Lord hath anointed me to preach good tidings unto the meek" (Isa. 61:1). The Holy Spirit is not just sent, but Himself sends the Son, who is sent by the Father. He is therefore shown to be the same as the Father and the Son in nature, power, operation and honour. By the good pleasure of the Father and the cooperation of the Holy Spirit, the only-begotten Son of God, on account of the boundless ocean of divine love for mankind, bowed down the heavens and came down (Ps. 18:9). He appeared on earth after our fashion, lived among us, and did and taught great, wonderful and sublime things truly worthy of God, which led those who obeyed Him towards deification and salvation.

After willingly suffering for our salvation, being buried and rising on the third day, He ascended into heaven and sat down on the right hand of the Father, whence He co-operated in the descent of the divine Spirit upon His disciples by sending down together with the Father the power from on high, as Both had promised (cf. Luke 24:49). Having sat down in the heavens, He seems to call to us from there, "If anyone wants to approach this glory, become a partaker of the kingdom of heaven, be called a son of God and find eternal life, inexpressible honour, pure joy and never-ending riches, let him heed My commandments and imitate as far as he can My own way of life. Let him follow My actions and teachings when I came to the world in the flesh to establish saving laws and offer Myself as a pattern." Truly the Saviour confirmed the gospel teaching by His deeds and miracles, and fulfilled it through His sufferings. He proved how beneficial it was for salvation by His resurrection from the dead, His ascension into heaven, and now by the descent of the divine Spirit upon His disciples, the event we celebrate today. After rising from the dead and appearing to

His disciples, He said as He was taken up into heaven, "Behold, I send the promise of my Father upon you: but tarry ye in the city of Jerusalem, until ye be endued with power from on high" (Luke 24:49). "For ye shall receive power, after that the Holy Ghost is come upon you: and ye shall be witnesses unto me both in Jerusalem, and in all Judaea, and unto the uttermost part of the earth" (cf. Acts 1:8).

When the fiftieth day after the resurrection had come, the day we now commemorate, all the disciples were gathered with one accord in the upper room, each having also gathered together his thoughts (for they were devoting themselves intently to prayer and hymns to God). "And suddenly", says Luke the evangelist, "there came a sound from heaven as of a rushing mighty wind, and it filled the house where they were sitting" (Acts 2:1–11). This is the sound which the prophetess Hannah foretold when she received the promise concerning Samuel: "The Lord went up to heaven and thundered; and he shall give strength and exalt the horn of his anointed" (cf. 1 Sam. 2:10 Lxx). Elijah's vision also forewarned of this sound: "Behold the voice of a light breeze, and in it was the Lord" (cf. 1 Kgs. 19:12 Lxx). This "voice of a light breeze" is the sound of breath. You might also find a reference to it in Christ's gospel. According to John the theologian and evangelist, "In the last day, that great day of the feast", that is to say Pentecost, "Jesus stood and cried, saying, If any man thirst, let him come unto me and drink . . . This spake he of the Spirit, which they that believe on him should receive" (John 7:37–39). Again, after His resurrection He breathed on His disciples and said, "Receive ye the Holy Ghost" (John 20:22).

That cry of Christ prefigured this sound, and His breathing upon the disciples foretold the breath, which is now poured down abundantly from above and resounds with a great voice heard far and wide, summoning everything under heaven, pouring grace over all who approach with faith and filling them with it. It is forceful in that it is all-conquering, storms the ramparts of evil, and destroys all the enemy's cities and strongholds. It brings low the proud and lifts up the humble in heart, binds what should not have been loosed, breaks the bonds of sins and undoes what is held fast. It filled the house where they were sitting, making it a spiritual font, and accomplishing the promise which the Saviour made them when He ascended, saying, "For John truly baptized with water; but ye shall be baptized with the Holy Ghost not many days hence" (Acts 1:5). Even the name which He gave them proved to be true, for through this noise from heaven the apostles actually became sons of Thunder (*cf.* Mark 3:17). "And there appeared unto them", it says, "cloven tongues like as of fire, and it sat upon each of them. And they were all filled with the Holy Ghost, and began to speak with other tongues, as the Spirit gave them utterance" (Acts 2:3–4).

Those miracles accomplished by the Lord in the flesh, which bore witness that He was God's only-begotten Son in His own person, united with us in the last days, came to an end. On the other hand, those wonders began which proclaimed the Holy Spirit as a divine person in His own right, that we might come to know and contemplate the great and venerable mystery of the Holy Trinity. The Holy Spirit had been active before: it was He who spoke through the prophets and proclaimed things to come. Later He worked through the disciples to drive out demons and heal diseases. But now He was manifested to all in His own person through the tongues of fire, and by sitting enthroned as Lord upon each of Christ's disciples, He made them instruments of His power.

Why did He appear in the form of tongues? It was to demonstrate that He shared the same nature as the Word of God, for there is no relationship closer than that between word and tongue. It was also because of teaching, since teaching Christ's gospel needs a tongue full of grace. But why fiery tongues? Not just because the Spirit is consubstantial with the Father and the Son – and our God is fire (*cf.* Heb. 12:29), a fire consuming wickedness – but also because of the twofold energy of the apostles' preaching, which can bring both benefit and punishment. As it is the property of fire to illuminate and burn, so Christ's teaching enlightens those who obey but finally hands over the disobedient to eternal fire and punishment. The text says, "tongues like fire" not "tongues of fire", that no one might imagine it was ordinary physical fire, but that we might understand the manifestation of the Spirit using fire as an example. Why did the tongues appear to be divided among them? Because the Spirit is given by measure by the Father to all except Christ (John 3:34), who Himself came from above. He, even in the flesh, possessed the fullness of divine power and energy, whereas the grace of the Holy Spirit was only partially, not fully, contained within anyone else. Each one obtained different gifts, lest anyone should suppose the grace given to the saints by the Holy Spirit was theirs by nature.

The fact that the divine Spirit sat upon them is proof not just of His lordly dignity, but of His unity. He sat, it says, "upon each of them. And they were all filled with the Holy Ghost" (Acts 2:3–4). For although divided in His various powers and energies, in each of His works the Holy Spirit is wholly present and active, undividedly divided, partaken of while remaining complete, like the sun's ray. They spoke with other tongues, other languages, to people from every nation, as the Spirit gave them utterance. They became instruments of the divine Spirit, inspired and motivated according to His will and power. Anything taken hold of by somebody outside itself, sharing in the energy but not the essence of the one acting through it, is his instrument. As David declared through the Holy Spirit, "My tongue is the pen of a ready writer" (Ps. 45:1). The pen is the writer's instrument, sharing in the energy, though obviously not the essence, of the writer, and inscribing whatever he wishes and is able to write.

In what sense is the Holy Spirit the promise of the Father? He foretold Him through His prophets, saying through Ezekiel, "A new heart also will I give you, and a new spirit will I put within you: and I will put my spirit within you" (*cf.* Ezek. 36:26–27). Through Joel He proclaims, "And it shall come to pass in the last days, that I will pour out my spirit upon all flesh" (*cf.* Joel 2:28). Longing for the Holy Spirit, Moses cried out in anticipation, "Would God that all the Lord's people were prophets, and that the Lord would put his spirit upon them" (Num. 11:29). As the gracious will of the Father and His promise are one and the same as the Son's, Christ told those who believed in Him, "Whosoever drinketh of the water that I shall give him, it shall be to him a well of water springing up into everlasting life" (cf. John 4:14), and, "He that believeth on me, as the scripture hath said, out of his belly shall flow rivers of living water" (John 7:38). By way of explanation, the evangelist says, "This spake He of the Spirit, which they that believe on him should receive" (John 7:39). As He approached His saving passion He told His disciples, "If ye love me, keep my commandments. And I will pray the Father, and he shall give you another Comforter, that he may abide with you for ever; even the Spirit of truth" (John 14:15–17). And again, "These things have I spoken unto you, being yet present with you. But the Comforter, which is the Holy Ghost, whom the Father will send in my name, he shall teach you all things" (John 14:25–26). And yet again, "When the Comforter is come, whom I will send unto you from the Father, even the Spirit of truth, which proceedeth from the Father, he shall testify of me" (John 15:26), and "he will guide you into all the truth" (John 16:13).

The promise was now fulfilled and the Holy Spirit, given and sent by both the Father and the Son, descended. He shone round about the holy disciples and with divine power kindled them all like lamps or, rather, He revealed them as heavenly lights set above the whole world, who had the word of eternal life, and through them He illuminated all the earth. If from one burning lamp someone lights another, then another from that one, and so on in succession, he has light continuously. In the same way, through the apostles ordaining their successors, and these successors ordaining others, and so on, the grace of the Holy Spirit is handed down through all generations and enlightens all who obey their spiritual shepherds and teachers.

Each hierarch in his turn comes to give the city this grace and gift of God and the enlightenment of the divine Spirit through the gospel. Those who reject any of them, as can happen, interrupt God's grace, break the divine succession, separate themselves from God and deliver themselves up to sinful rebellions and all kinds of disasters, as you are obviously aware from recent experience. If, however, now that you have returned to the shepherd of your souls appointed by God, you obey my counsels for salvation, you will really and truly celebrate this annual commemoration of the coming of the divine Spirit, who of His unimaginable love descended for our salvation, just as the only-begotten Son of God, because of this same love and for the same purpose, bowed the heavens, came down and assumed our flesh.

Christ had ascended bodily into heaven, so if He had not sent His Holy Spirit to accompany and strengthen His disciples and their successors in following generations who taught the gospel of grace, He would not have been preached to all nations, nor would the proclamation have been passed down to us. That is why the Lord, in His all-surpassing love for mankind, showed at Pentecost that His disciples were partakers, fathers and ministers of everlasting light and life, who bring us to new birth for eternal life and make those who are worthy children of the light and fathers of enlightenment. Thus, He Himself is with us unto the end of the world, as was promised through the Spirit (Matt. 28:20). For He is one with the Father and the Spirit, not according to hypostasis, but in His divinity, and God is one in three, in one tri-hypostatic and almighty divinity. The Holy Spirit always existed and was with the Son in the Father. How could the Father and divine Mind be without beginning if the Son and Word were not also without beginning? How could there be a pre-eternal Word without there also being a pre-eternal Spirit? Thus the Holy Spirit ever was and is and will be, co-Creator with the Father and the Son, together with them renewing that which has suffered corruption, and sustaining the things that endure. He is everywhere present and fills, directs and oversees everything. "Whither shall I go from thy spirit", says the psalmist to God, "Or whither shall I flee from thy presence?" (Ps. 139:7).

He is not just everywhere, but also above all, not just in every age and time, but before them all. And, according to the promise, the Holy Spirit will not just be with us until the end of the age, but rather will stay with those who are worthy in the age to come, making them immortal and filling their bodies as well with eternal glory, as the Lord indicated by telling His disciples, "I will pray the Father, and he shall give you another Comforter, that he may abide with you for ever" (John 14:16). "It is sown", says the apostle (meaning buried and committed to the earth), "a dead natural body", that is to say, an ordinary created body with a created soul, stable and capable of movement. "It is raised" (that is, comes back to life), "a spiritual body" (*cf.* 1 Cor. 15:44), which means a supernatural body, framed and ordered by the Holy Spirit, and clothed in immortality, glory and incorruption by the Spirit's power (*cf.* 1 Cor. 15:53). "The first man, Adam", he says, "was made a living soul; the last Adam was made a quickening spirit. The first man is of the earth, earthy; the second man is the Lord from heaven. As is the earthy, such are they also that are earthy: and as is the heavenly, such are they also that are heavenly" (*cf.* 1 Cor. 15:45, 47–48).

Who are these heavenly people? Those who are steadfast and immovable in their faith, who always abound in the Lord's work and bear the image of the heavenly Adam through their obedience to Him. "He that obeyeth not the Son", says John, the Lord's Forerunner, through John the evangelist, "shall not see life; but the wrath of God abideth on him" (John 3:36). Who can endure God's wrath? "It is a fearful thing", brethren, "to fall into the hands of the living God" (Heb. 10:31). If we fear the hands of our enemies, even though the Lord says, "fear not them which kill the body" (Matt. 10:28), who in his right mind will not fear God's hands raised in anger against the disobedient? For the wrath of God will be revealed against everyone who lives impurely and unjustly without repenting and holds the truth in unrighteousness (Rom. 1:18).

Let us flee from wrath and hasten through repentance to obtain the kindness and compassion of the divine Spirit. If anyone feels hatred towards another, let him be reconciled with him and restore love, lest his hatred and conflict with his brother should bear witness against him that he does not love God. "For if you do not love your brother whom you have seen, how can you love God whom you have not seen?" (*cf.* 1 John 4:20). When we love one another, let our love be unfeigned, and let us show it in deeds, by neither saying nor doing, nor even enduring to hear, anything insulting or harmful to our brethren. As Christ's beloved theologian taught us, "Brethren, do not love in word, neither in tongue; but in deed and in truth" (*cf.* 1 John 3:18).

Anyone who has fallen into fornication, adultery or any other such bodily impurity, should desist from this revolting filth and cleanse himself through confession, tears, fasting and the like. For God judges unrepentant fornicators and adulterers. He condemns them, dismisses them and consigns them to hell, unquenchable fire and other never-ending punishments, saying, "Let the impure and accursed be taken away, lest they see and enjoy the glory of the Lord" (*cf.* Isa. 26:10 Lxx). Let thieves and all who are openly grasping and greedy stop stealing, defrauding and seizing what belongs to others, but also share their own possessions with those in need. In a word, if you desire life, to see good days, to be rescued from enemies both visible and invisible, the barbarians currently threatening us, and those punishments reserved for the prince of evil and his angels, depart from all evil and do good (Ps. 34:12, 14). "Be not deceived", the apostle tells the Corinthians, "neither fornicators, nor adulterers, nor effeminate, nor abusers of themselves with men, nor covetous, neither drunkards nor revilers, nor extortioners, shall inherit the kingdom of God" (*cf.* 1 Cor. 6:9–10). If someone has no inheritance with God he neither belongs to God nor has God as his Father.

But let us, brethren, I beseech you, abstain from deeds and words hateful to God, that we may boldly call God our Father. Let us truly return to Him, that He too may turn back to us, cleanse us from all sin and make us worthy of His divine grace. Then shall we keep festival both now and for ever, and celebrate in a godly and spiritual way the accomplishments of God's promise, the coming of the All-holy Spirit among men and His resting upon them; the fulfillment and perfection of the blessed hope in Christ Himself our Lord.

For to Him belong glory, honour and worship, with His Father without beginning and the all-holy, good and life-giving Spirit, now and for ever and unto the ages of ages. Amen.